COLE FOSTER

AND

STYLE. SUBSTANCE.

COLE FOSTER WITH MIKE LaVELLA
FOREWORD BY KIRK HAMMETT

motorbooks

TO MY BEST FRIEND, MY DAD.

First published in 2008 by Motorbooks, an imprint of MBI Publishing Company, 400 First Avenue North, Suite 300, Minneapolis, MN 55401 USA

Motorbooks titles are also available at discounts in bulk quantity for industrial or sales-promotional use. For details write to Special Sales Manager at MBI Publishing Company, 400 First Avenue North, Suite 300, Minneapolis, MN 55401 USA.

To find out more about our books, join us online at www.motorbooks.com.

Library of Congress Cataloging-in-Publication Data

Foster, Cole, 1964–
    Cole Foster and Salinas Boyz Customs : style, substance / by Cole Foster with Mike LaVella.
        p. cm.
    Includes index.
    ISBN 978-0-7603-3167-5 (hb w/ jkt)
    1. Automobile engineers—United States—Biography. 2. Hot rods—California. 3. Automobiles—Customizing—California. 4. Motorcycles—Customizing—California. 5. Salinas Boyz Customs. I. LaVella, Mike, 1964– II. Title. III. Title: Cole Foster and Salinas Boyz Customs.
    TL140.F67A3 2008
    629.28'7092—dc22

2008005749

Front cover: Blue steel. Cole with his '52 Panhead and the blue '54. *Jesus Espinoza, DeadendMagazine.com*

Frontispiece: Would you let your daughter date this man? *Mike Chase*

Title pages: At the old shop . . . with no shortage of projects. *David Perry*

Outro: Another one on the books. *David Perry*

Back cover: Behold, the art of the bobber. Hamming it up in a Salinas lettuce field.

Editor: Dennis Pernu
Designer: Cindy Samargia Laun

Printed in China

CONTENTS

FOREWORD

MAESTRO OF THE WRENCH AND WELD

My appreciation of four-wheeled vehicles started when I was five years old, cruising down the 101 with my father. He had a silver-green '67 GTO that was his pride and joy, and his enthusiasm was so great that it rubbed off on my impressionable young mind instantly. My mom had a Corvair, and I realized that, compared to Mom's car, Dad's GTO was the one that meant business.

As I got older I was drawn to my brother's "Big Daddy" Roth models because they combined hot rods with my other obsession: horror and monster movies. That grew into building my own car models, collecting Hot Wheels, racing AFX slot cars, and attempting to build my own go-kart. It was then that I realized that my wrenching abilities were not quite on par with my friends', but that didn't stop me in my teens from trying to rebuild a beaten-up Ford Capri motor with a friend. At the end of the rebuild I had all these spare nuts and bolts and couldn't figure out why. Needless to say, once we started the engine (that was a surprise!) and put it

into drive, it ran about a block before seizing up, belching a bunch of black smoke, and finally gasping its last breath. From that point on I made the decision to leave the mechanical duties to someone else, but my love of automobiles never left me.

Which brings me to Cole. I always wanted a custom rod. I always marveled at the sleek machines I saw on the street, in magazines, and in my travels, and I fantasized about being behind the wheel of one of these metallic beauties. But then I would remember my frustrations with my mechanical abilities and think that I could never build one for myself. Maybe someday . . .

Then I met Cole backstage at a ZZ Top concert. Billy F Gibbons introduced us. Cole and I hit it off instantly and decided right there that maybe he could build something for me. When I went to his garage in Salinas, I was just blown away by his work. This guy could build anything! And we came from the same generation that loved the old-school guys like George Barris. We agreed that he would build me something not quite as flamboyant, but understated and stylish, dark and threatening at the same time. What Cole created two years later was far better than I ever imagined: a super-customized '36 Ford that had a look like no other. He took the initial vision much further than I expected, creating a highly conceptual moving piece of art that continues to blow me away so much that it doesn't seem real, like something you would only see in a daydream.

Cole is the ultimate in my book. A true artist. A maestro of the wrench and weld. A man with an unstoppable vision. The best that I have known.

Kirk Hammett
Paris, France
July 2007

Cole and Kirk at the 2007 Grand National Roadster Show.
Cole & Susan Foster collection

Kirk's '36 Ford three-window. *Jesus Espinoza, DeadendMagazine.com*

CHAPTER ONE

STORY OF

I didn't know it at the time, but I grew up in the hub of cool: the San Fernando Valley. The Valley is made up of a bunch of little cities just outside L.A.—Van Nuys, Reseda, Woodland Hills, Canoga Park, Northridge, Tarzana. After World War II, some of the best pinstripers, painters, customizers, and hot rod builders came out of there. Later, there was drag racing, skateboarding, minibikes, and go-karts, not to mention surfing just over the hill in Malibu.

But, like I said, not knowing anything else, I didn't really appreciate it at the time. When I was sixteen and moved to Northern California with my dad, I may as well have been dropped into the middle of Czechoslovakia. What was cool and new just did not spread within seconds like it does today with cable TV and the Internet. But more on Nor-Cal later.

I was born in Van Nuys in 1964 and my family lived about five miles away on a dead-end street in Tarzana. You took a little dirt road to get to our place. The Valley back then was rural—all big trees and orchards—and most people had horses and a couple of acres. My best friends were a few girls from the "neighborhood" and a Mexican family that lived down the road. It was a fairly

Cole at one and a half, 1965.
Cole & Susan Foster collection

normal place, really, but I didn't care about anything except going to the drag races. It was what my father, Pat Foster, did, but I really didn't realize how special that was until I was a little older and more social in school—you know, sharing crayons and talking to other kids about what their fathers did for a living.

My dad was a driver and a chassis builder. He built racecars for B&M in the 1960s and worked with legendary guys like Woody Gilmore, Ronnie Scrima, Frank Huszar, Jim Hume, John Buttera, Nye Frank, and Tom Jobe. He even had a full-time gig building Mickey Thompson's land-speed-record car and driving his Funny Cars.

Left: A future builder learns about pre-1961 Grand Prix cars. *Right:* Terrorizing the streets of Tarzana, 1967. *Cole & Susan Foster collection*

The Fosters are English-Irish, so they could've been in America for quite a while, but it's hard to know for sure. My grandfather Art was from Kansas and moved to Oregon before coming to California. He wasn't college educated, but he ended up an engineer in the aircraft industry. My dad's brother Birch attended UCLA and enlisted in the army. He never graduated college, but worked for an early computer company and moved up the ladder to vice president. With my dad's side of the family, there's always a Scrabble game going and they're big on crossword puzzles. Sharp people.

Once, when I was five, we were in Long Beach watching go-kart races, when a minibike zoomed by. My dad asked me which I liked best, the go-karts or the minibike? I said I liked the go-karts. One day soon after, Dad told me to go get something out of his pickup for him. I went out and there was a new go-kart in the pickup box.

DEAR COLE & DANNY & YOU MOM ..
I MISS YOU ALL VERY MUCH & I THOUGHT IT WAS TIME TO WRITE & TELL YOU SO. I AM SORRY I MADE YOU CRY THE OTHER NITE WHEN I CALLED & TALKED TO YOU ALL, BUT SOMETIMES I HAVE TO TELL YOU GUYS TO BE GOOD & HELP YOUR MOTHER, CAUSE I THINK SOMETIMES YOU JUST FORGET HOW MUCH I LOVE AND TRUST YOU
DADDY HAS BEEN DOING REAL WELL WITH THE RACE CAR, WINNING AND GOING FAST & QUICK I AM HAVING A GOOD TIME EVEN THOUGH I WISH I WERE HOME WITH YOU MORE. THE LAST TWO DAYS I'VE BEEN IN PENN. STAYING WITH

Dad checks in from the road. For a six-year-old, it doesn't get much heavier than this. *Cole & Susan Foster collection*

A FRIEND OF MINE WHO'S NAME IS "JUNGLE" JIM LIBERMAN. HE HAS A RACE CAR TOO. FROM HERE WE GO TO OHIO FOR A RACE AGAINST THE ~~CHI-TOWN~~ "CHI-TOWN HUSTLER" WHO RUNS AS GOOD AS ANYONE IN THE COUNTRY, IT'LL BE A TOUGH ONE TO WIN. HAVE MOM SHOW YOU ON A MAP WHERE PENN & OHIO ARE. HAVE SAY GOODBYE NOW, HAVE TO GO WASH SOME CLOTHES. SAY HELLO TOO EVERY ONE FOR ME PLEASE. YOU GUYS BE GOOD BOYS TILL I CAN FLY HOME & SEE YOU, THAT'LL BE SOON I HOPE. LOVE YOU ALL SO VERRY VERRY MUCH YOUR DAD Pat —

It had a Hodaka 90 in it and was something a kid four or five years older might drive. Sure enough, Dad got it from Woody Gilmore, whose kid was ten years older than me; they had built it for him to race. It arrived just as the new street was laid in front of our house—a dead end with a power company on one side and no driveways except ours on the whole block. It was like having a private racetrack right in Tarzana. I was in first grade, so the go-kart was intimidating and it got going good. Dad taught me how to handle it, to slide around turns, applying the brakes only when necessary. A year or so later, he brought home some dirt bikes and he'd take me and my younger brother Dan for some wild rides. We rode a lot, but I was always a little more timid than my brother. I don't know if he was just younger and dumber, but he was fearless.

In the summer of 1970, when I was six and Dan was only four, Dad took a job in Chicago driving for Chris "The Greek" Karamesines. We all packed into our VW Bug and drove straight through from sunny California to the mean streets of Chicago. It was a gnarly ride, with Dad drafting right on the bumpers of eighteen-wheelers. I remember waking up at one point to flares, lights, and sirens, and my mom Carolynn telling us to "keep our heads down," which of course just piqued my curiosity. It was like when we were at an R-rated movie at the drive-in and breasts came on the screen—the more they say "Get down," the more you just know it's something good. In this case, it was a car that was hit by a train and flattened like a pancake. Maybe that time I shouldn't have looked.

We stayed in a little guest cottage behind The Greek's house on the South Side. There we were—my little brother and me from this cul-de-sac in Tarzana, dropped right into Chicago. We got our asses kicked the very first day. City life was definitely rough, and the South Side of Chicago is about as tough as it gets. I remember a kid next door who was about my age asking me what my dad did. I said, "He drives racecars." He said, "My dad robs people."

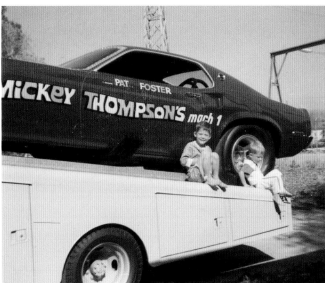

Top left: Kindergarten, 1968–1969. *Cole & Susan Foster collection*

Left: The summer of 1969. Cole and brother Dan with Dad's ride. Pat Foster's teammate that year, Danny Ongais, drove a blue version of the *Mickey Thompson Mach 1* Mustang. Both were built by Pat. *Cole & Susan Foster collection*

The Greek had kids who were older than us, including a daughter named Paula who I adored. Generally, they were crazy. They weren't old enough to drive cars, but they had go-karts and minibikes that they drove on the streets. They would send me to the liquor store with a note from a fictitious aunt to get them cigarettes and a bottle of booze. I guess they picked me because I was only six and therefore more likely to pull it off. The store did serve me every time.

One day we were in the Greek's utility shed and the neighbor girl talked me into lighting an old tennis shoe on fire with a pack of matches she had. Once it got going good, we did what all kids do: We ran. And, as is usually the case, we got caught. The Greek was really pissed, and I was grounded for a few weeks, but all in all, it was a fun summer.

When I was nine, we moved a couple miles away to Reseda, which was a little more of a real neighborhood with track houses and everything. My mom had a best friend right across the street, so even though I switched schools, I knew the local kids because we had visited often.

In the summer of 1970, Pat Foster took a job driving for Chicago-based Chris "The Greek" Karamesines. That's Cole and Dan with the Greek's daughter, Paula. Chicago's South Side was an eye-opening experience for a kid from the Valley. *Cole & Susan Foster collection*

Summer, 1971. How many kids had a world-class Funny Car fabricator/driver available to tune their go-kart? Two, for certain. *Cole & Susan Foster collection*

With mom Carolynn, Christmas, 1971. *Cole & Susan Foster collection*

LOOKING BACK ON MY SON'S LIFE

makes me a very proud mother. I knew he had a talent at a very early age. Cole was a very inventive child. When he was twelve he went to his dad's shop and made a rocket plane out of wood and aluminum. He then tied it to streetlight poles and shot it off down the block to the cheers of the whole neighborhood. He was drawing crowds then and continues to do so today.

He has been a wonderful son whom I love very much.

—Carolynn Foster-Novak

Fifth grade, 1973–1974. *Cole & Susan Foster collection*

My mom's maiden name is Coleman. The Colemans were from Van Nuys, where my grandmother Laverne was a beauty queen in the 1920s. My grandfather, Ellis, was an eccentric guy and a very skillful carpenter. I have a picture of him when he was probably seventeen, working on the L.A. Coliseum for the 1932 Olympics. He ended up working for the movie studios, first Disney, then Universal. He was head of the back lot, where they have the Western and city sets, but Grandpa wasn't a spoiler, so we didn't go to the studio a bunch. I do remember going there once and riding around in the Jeep with him. Later, he built his own cabin up in Frasier Park and we'd go there often. He was hands-on. He even built his own swimming pool at his house.

If you looked at our house in Reseda, you'd never know anyone involved with racing lived there—no racecar trailer in the driveway, no mailbox with flames on it. Dad even drove a VW Bug. The house was pretty, the grass was cut, and that was that. So 1975, the summer that dad drove a Funny Car sponsored by Chapman Automotive and the Chicago Police Department, really stands out. The car, called the *Chicago Patrol*, was based out of the Midwest, but the team was on tour on the West Coast when it needed to be serviced. It was the only time that Dad worked on a car at home. It was there for two weeks, right in the driveway, with the body on the lawn. The crew took over the garage. You know the neighborhood kids who say, "My dad's Camaro could beat yours"? When they saw the car, I was king of the neighborhood, at least for two weeks. We almost had to rope off the front lawn to keep kids out. Once, Dad and the crew lit it off in the driveway and it shot flames over the roof.

I really looked forward to going to the races, and the older I got, the more I wanted to be a driver. I did get to travel some with the cars, and those were great years to do it. Drag racing was a real gladiator sport, full of colorful characters. Even though the ETs are two seconds quicker now than they were in those days, I think it was better. It was very glamorous, very cool. The Snake and Mongoose were larger than life. Like all kids, I saw them on TV and had their Hot Wheels set, but I got to

know them in real life too. They'd come over to our house. They were my heroes, along with Pops. He was right there with them.

Sometimes I traveled with the car for the whole summer. I had to grow up and be my own little self-sufficient man, getting my own meals and things like that, because you could not be a little puss on the road. At night, the parking lots of the hotels that the drivers stayed at were like pits. These guys worked on their cars all night long. They had generators going and lights everywhere. It was like a carnival—surreal but very neat. At a Holiday Inn in Tulsa, Oklahoma, one crazy night when I was eight or nine years old, Don Garlits was out there at midnight beating on his car, which was completely torn down. I just sat there watching him and he asked, "What are you doing here, kid?"

I said, "I'm here with my dad." He just kept working, but I asked "You got any pictures or stickers?"

"No, not with me. Is your old man a racer?"

"Yeah, Pat."

"Foster?"

I nodded, and he said, "Your dad is a hell of a racer. I really respect him." Then he said, "Come here, kid" and went to his trailer and gave me his press kit, a Pee-Chee folder with glossies in it. I still have it. I have some great memories of those times and just hanging out with legends like Garlits.

In the pits with Dad, Summer 1978. Pat took over as shoe midyear. *Cole & Susan Foster collection*

As with a lot of kids growing up in the 1970s, bicycles were a huge part of Cole's youth. "We worked on them every day . . . mixed and matched parts." It looks like young Cole's getting a bit crossed-up in midair. *Cole & Susan Foster collection*

Around 1972, Pat Foster and other drag racing notables like Don Prudhomme and John Buttera began racing dirt bikes recreationally at Indian Dunes, where this photo was taken. Cole remembers meeting Steve McQueen in the pits there. Note Dan's Ed Pink Racing Engines tee and the bike in the background. *Cole & Susan Foster collection*

The last and most prestigious race of the year was in Indianapolis. It was always on Labor Day, but I had to be back home in a couple days for the start of school. That got rougher as I got older. I just wanted to be at the races. During the school year I went mostly to drag strips in Southern California—Long Beach, Orange County, Irwindale, and the Ontario Motor Speedway. Dad would always qualify and sometimes break records weekly, and there we'd be in the winner's circle.

I wouldn't have traded my gold-plated backstage pass to drag racing for anything. I didn't actually stop at the Grand Canyon like most fifth-graders on summer vacation, but my what-I-did-this-summer stories almost made my teachers faint, like John "Tarzan" Austin shooting a .44 out the truck window and throwing half-sticks of TNT onto the highway for us to dodge. Those guys were in their twenties with pockets full of cash—women adored them and locals feared them. They're still my heroes. Today, I can't even imagine being in my twenties, driving a Funny Car, and traveling around the country like they did—rock stars who didn't have to stuff their jeans, because there was no question what those boys were packing.

Back in Reseda, bicycles ruled everything. The neighborhood bicycle builds began to run neck and neck with the races, because I was actually working on the

bikes. With racing I was a spectator, just taking it all in until later, but the bicycle thing was dead serious, probably as competitive as custom car shows are for adults now. We worked on them every day. We didn't have the means to totally customize them, but we did the best we could. Everyone started with a Sting-ray, then mixed and matched parts. For example, you would go to a Honda shop and get motocross bars, but then you'd have to sweet talk some old guy at the Dodge dealership behind our house to pry open your gooseneck, put the new bars in, and then squeeze them down and braze them because they were the wrong size.

It evolved constantly. One summer you'd run a slick with a cruiser seat, the next year you had to have a metal-flake banana seat high in the front and lowered all the way down to the chrome fender in the back. And it had to be right. The paint jobs were always a big deal with us. We sanded and primered the bikes, then went to Pep Boys and bought metallic automotive lacquer touchup paint—

not candy, but close. We did fades, like orange to red, all with spray cans. We were also into wheelies, ramp-to-ramp jumps, and sliding.

We covered a lot of ground on those bikes. In Reseda, the L.A. River Basin—the "wash"—was right behind us, where they filmed movies like *Grease*. When you see them racing the two jalopies in the wash, well, that was our own super freeway. Huge overflow tunnels ran off the wash like fingers, and we would get inside and ride to the other side of the Valley. It took all of us to lift up the big iron grate and then prop it up with one bike while the rest of us went on in. Once you got inside, it was pitch black, so you had to have a flashlight. It was wild, man. We'd go for ten miles or so then peek up through the gutters to see where we were. Later, when we had motorcycles, I rode our RM80 through the wash because you were untouchable. The police just couldn't get to you.

Before we got real dirt bikes, though, we had a Rupp minibike with a five-horsepower motor and full suspension. Pretty good. But when the local kids started getting little two-stroke motocross bikes around 1978, the minibike was just not happening. Luckily, Don Prudhomme was sponsored by Suzuki, and they gave him an RM80 to use as pit bike. After that season, Dad brought the Snake's Suzuki home for us. It had a dent in the tank. Apparently, they ran out of gas on the road somewhere and had to put a five-gallon metal gas can on top of the tank and ride it to a station. Other than that dent, it was like brand new and had never seen the dirt.

My dad and a lot of the other drag-racing guys had started buying dirt bikes around 1972 and riding them at places like Holiday Hills and Indian Dunes. They all started out with Yamaha 185s but graduated quickly to Huskies and Maicos. I went out there but not really to ride because I was still young. I'd ride the minibike in the pit area. Prudhomme, Buttera, and Ed Pink had bikes, and guys like Don Moody and Ed "The Ace" McCulloch were there too. They were all as competitive in the dirt as they were at the track; a few of them really got hurt trying to outdo each other. They were wild times. In fact, Steve McQueen rode with them a little bit. I met him there in the pits.

I was an okay dirt biker, perhaps the baddest on my block. But then I'd go to a real track and see the kids with brand new bikes who practiced every day, and I just

"I wouldn't have traded my gold-plated backstage pass to drag racing for anything." At the wheel of the *Super Shops Arrow* as it gets towed to the line, August 1978. *Cole & Susan Foster collection*

wasn't that guy. I was just a kid from Reseda who had a dirt bike. I was lucky if I could get out to the desert to ride a couple times a year. That was until a kid named Jimmy Hartman, who had a Superdad, moved in down the street. They built a Baja Bug together and he had a brand new water-cooled Honda 125. I went to the races with him a few times and thought, "I can do this." So I showed up with my hand-me-down leathers, signed up, and got a number. I wasn't scared, but my bike was a couple of years older than everyone else's and some of these guys were pros. The green flag dropped, and I fell behind; I'd never ridden on a big international track before, and I didn't even know what was coming around the next turn. It was crazy to even be out there, but I thought I was doing OK. On about the third lap, a kid passed me on a jump and turned around and waved.

A few hours later when the flag dropped on the final moto, I got a great hole shot and was up front, but I think it was worse than being in the back.

I loved motocross. Marty Smith and Bob Hannah were my heroes. I really would have liked to race, but it just wasn't to be. Of course, something else occupied the rest of my time: skateboarding.

Cole recalls that skateboards pretty much displaced the Sting-rays around 1977. Skating also offered Cole an entrée with a new crew when he moved to Carmel with his dad. This photo was taken around 1988. *Cole & Susan Foster collection*

In our neighborhood, bicycles were done by 1977 when Sims came out with Road Rider wheels. It was the turning point for skating everywhere. Before that we all had stupid Black Knight skateboards that weren't very fun to ride, but when the good urethane wheels came out it was back on. One day we heard rumors that they were building a skate park less than a mile down the street from where we lived. They started the construction, but we still weren't really sure that it was real until we saw them form those banks. It was like a dream come true— SkaterCross was probably the best skate park around, and it was right down the street. When it finally opened, the first day was total pageantry. They invited pros, and they all showed up in matching team colors, like what you'd see in a made-for-TV movie about skateboarding or on an episode of *CHiPS*.

Then the Dogtown skaters showed up. This was right when *Skateboarder* magazine came out, and we had seen them all in there. Now here they were, bigger than life itself: Jim "Red Dog" Muir, Stacy Peralta, and all those

guys. But Tony Alva was the star for sure. I asked him, "Hey, are you Tony Alva?" He looked me straight in the eye and said, "Nope," and just walked right by. Looking back now, that was cool, but at the time I didn't think so.

Jay Adams was always supercool and definitely the best skateboarder we'd ever seen. He would show up in his street clothes without a skateboard, wear rental stuff, and just rule the place. You could always tell that guy had something that the rest of them didn't. I got to meet him years later after moving up to Carmel. I was at a surf contest and someone said, "Jay Adams wants to meet you." My chopped Chevy was there, and it turned out he was into cars, so we B.S.'d for a while and hit it off. It's nice when your heroes end up being cool guys. Sometimes it's better not to meet them, but in his case, it was great.

One time in the summer of 1979, I went down to the youth center because I heard there was something going on, which turned out to be a weekend-long thing with punk bands playing. I went inside and saw The

Chiefs. I never liked Van Halen—I was always more into bands like Blondie and Cheap Trick and Devo. But all the stoner guys I hung around with in junior high loved Rush and never shut up about Neil Peart, so I was the outcast in my group. I changed schools right about then when we moved a few miles away to Woodland Hills. The kids there knew a lot more about punk rock than the Reseda boys. After that, I listened to the Rodney show on KROQ, which is where I first heard bands like Social Distortion, The Adolescents, and X. One day I found out that X was playing at the Starwood. I wanted to go, but I'd never even been to Hollywood. I was a kid stuck out in the Valley without a car. My friend Kyle Tyson's older brother TK offered to take me if I bought him a ticket. TK was a classic stoner guy who probably stills lives at home. He was an expert on music and weed who played a little guitar and drove a '69 Mustang that was never registered. He'd take backstreets everywhere, driving really slowly, but we made it to the Starwood. When X went on, it was a trip. I'd never heard anything like "White Girl" before. From then on, punk rock was it.

We had lived in Reseda until I was thirteen, then my mom and dad got divorced. I split my time between them, eventually moving in with my dad in Van Nuys. He was driving the Super Shops Funny Car, which was kept in a garage behind Ed Pink Racing Engines. That was a cool place—Don Prudhomme and Shirley Muldowney were also there. I would ride my bike down there every day after school, working first as the cleanup kid, and then later on the Funny Car, which mostly stayed on the West Coast. A typical deal would be to race at, say, Orange County on the weekend, then on Monday the body would come off and be on barrels for me after school. I would spray the whole underneath with degreaser and scrape the rubber off, then wash and wax it and restock the trailer. That was my deal for a few hours after school. They even paid me. At this point I really had my heart set on racing for a living.

Then Dad met a lady named Leslie, and off to Woodland Hills we went. I did a year of high school there before Leslie became my stepmom and Dad announced that he was done with racing and we moved north to Carmel Valley on the Monterey Peninsula. With no friends, no bands, no good radio, and my dreams of racing gone, it was as if the rug got jerked out from under me.

Ninth-grade graduation, 1978. *Cole & Susan Foster collection*

It was a rough time to move. In Woodland Hills, I had just started having girlfriends. My whole social thing was just forming and then "Great, another new school." I was sixteen years old, just getting my driver's license, and two years away from going into racing full-time.

Dad certainly wasn't a has-been when he quit. In fact, he was on top of the world. He was the third driver to make the 5-Second Club, which was a big deal. He had just broken the track record at Fremont and won the Western Championship. I thought I was going to slide right into the whole racing thing. But you have to have thick skin in drag racing, especially when you're a hired driver like Dad. You can show up to work one day and your name is wiped off the car. I don't know what exactly happened, but I think it was better for me that Dad just said, "We're going to move."

In the winner's circle at Seattle: Wolfy, Cole, Bernie, and Pat. In April 1979, Cole's dad made a 5.99-second pass in the *Super Shops Arrow*, becoming the third Funny Car driver to earn a spot in the Cragar 5-Second Club. *Cole & Susan Foster collection*

So there I was in Carmel Valley with my dad and his new wife. My brother Dan and mom stayed in L.A. We had raced at Fremont before and would stop for a night in Carmel or Big Sur, so it was a place I liked to visit, but I didn't think I'd ever live there. It was quite a change from the Valley. Dad did have a good opportunity in Carmel Valley: His friend, the architect Rob Carver, put him to work building a house for him, then one for a

steelmaker named Ken Minotti. I'm talking about building every door handle and hinge from scratch.

Leslie and I had our own issues, her being twenty-three and me sixteen. She was the one who prompted Dad to quit racing; he probably wouldn't have told me so that I couldn't hold it against her. For almost five years, Dad and I didn't talk about racing at all. I would think, "I'm going to call Lil' John Buttera and see if I can go race with him next summer," but I had to go to high school and I didn't have enough experience working on cars to be really needed.

Before we moved north, besides racing my other interest was art. I wanted to be a "real" painter, a fine artist. Painting and drawing were a big deal for me, and I thought I was really good until the tenth grade. I was pressured to draw for the yearbook staff. It was run by a really cool teacher who sent me to a seminar at one of the big old high schools in downtown L.A. We watched their theater class put on a political drama, then we were put in a room and asked to draw a political cartoon of our take on it. Other kids drew cartoons that could have been in *The New Yorker*. It was completely over my head. I just drew a Funny Car! I really had to try—those kids just had it.

I did my junior and senior years at Carmel High School. It seemed like ten years behind the times. Everyone listened to AC/DC, and I was listening to the Ramones and Sex Pistols. Luckily, skaters were the same wherever you went, so I'd be wearing a punk rock T-shirt with Vans slip-ons, and they'd ask, "Do you skateboard? I have a ramp." That's how I met my first round of friends up here, like Noah Greenberg and Tim Connelly. Some of the kids had half-pipes, and sometimes we went to Santa Cruz to skate the pools after school.

But I was still the weirdo, too. There was no MTV yet, which later equalized the world, but there was a show called *MV3* that had crappy bands like Missing Persons, almost like a dance show. It was way too safe. These kids were so behind the times. Real punk rock? They never heard of it. So I turned some guys on to punk. I had friends back in L.A. who sent me tapes, or I would go down to visit my mom and Dan and pick stuff up. A couple of years later, Black Flag played in Monterey. Eventually, there was a little bit of action going on.

But at first, it was tough, especially culturally. Kids up here just smoked weed and talked about Bon Scott dying—it was bad. Carmel had much more of a drug culture, too—small town plus rich kids equals the perfect element for dope. There was certainly no SkaterCross down the street, so they smoked weed. There was always a lot of pot around. Most teachers at Carmel High were leftover hippies, so in ceramics class, of course, the kids made bongs. But I never was a big smoker, or drinker for that matter. I guess I've always had a built-in safety system that gives me a headache or makes me sick before I can get too loaded. For the most part, the girls liked me but the guys were—well, let me put it this way: You couldn't make the baseball team because it was picked ten years ago when they all played Little League together. In some ways it was like a little bubble that you couldn't get into, but with chicks, it was like shooting fish in a barrel.

I was sixteen, I had my driver's license, and I had a car. All I needed was a job. I started working at a seafood restaurant in Carmel, bussing tables and washing dishes for $3.35 an hour. I got the car for my ninth-grade graduation—my mom gave me her old '77 Vega, a little pumpkin-orange GT. Everything was clean, but the motor was junk, so while I was working at Ed Pink's, the mechanic there built a motor that I helped put in. When we moved, Dad said, "Get a job, get insurance, and it's yours." I really needed it, being stuck out in Carmel Valley where there was one little Safeway store and nothing else. The beach was six or seven miles away. That summer, even though I was still in semi-shock, I thought, "I better get my act together," so I did.

There I was, the new kid at school again. Luckily, another guy named Will Karges happened to move up from L.A. at the same time. We were about the same speed. Compared to these kids, I could relate to him. My dad drove racecars, his dad owned racecars. We were pretty hip musically. He was a surfer from Malibu, I was a skateboarder from the Valley. For us, Carmel High was like stepping back in time. It was completely snow white, there was only one half-black kid there, plus I went from being in a school with over four thousand kids to a graduating class of less than a hundred. Even though it was little, in some ways it started to get very cool. For instance, the girls liked Will and me, coming from L.A. We were popular because they'd been with the same old guys for ages.

When Dad was building one of the custom houses, he got a shop in Sand City, a small industrial pocket on the Monterey Peninsula by the beach right outside of Carmel. Right next door to him was Dave Smith, who painted Rolls-Royces and high-end stuff. The kids working at the body shop were into cars too and we became friends. Dave gave me the key to his shop, and that's where I started doing bodywork.

CHAPTER TWO

ENTER THE SALINAS BOYS

I graduated in 1982 and moved into a tiny studio apartment fifteen miles out in Carmel Valley. I lived there for years, working and goofing around at Dave's body shop. Sometimes, I drove up to shows in San Francisco to see the Cramps, the Mentors, Flipper, the Dead Kennedys. I also saw Social Distortion way back then. Sometime around then I bought a BMW 2002.

Dad lived in Northern California for a year or two after I finished high school, and then moved to Dallas, Texas, to build racecars, this time for Raymond Beadle and the *Blue Max* team. It was 1984, and they were coming off a world championship, but I stayed in California. By then, I had my own little social scene. Remember, I was a big fish in a small pond. I had a steady girlfriend and was doing well, but when I went to visit Dad at Christmas, one of the guys asked me to come work on the car. I wasn't sure I still wanted to work in racing, but I decided to give it a go. It was a tough decision, especially leaving my girlfriend. In my heart, I didn't know if I was doing the right thing.

My job was prepping a new car for the upcoming season. We got it ready and went to the first few races, but I could tell that the crew chief, Dale Emery, didn't want me there. He had someone else in mind for the job, so he had a chip on his shoulder. But one guy on the team, Dee Gant, who used to work with my dad, thought I was a good kid and lobbied for me to work for them. It was funny—I used to look up to these guys. They came to dinner at my house when I was a kid and everything, but now they treated me completely differently. What a disappointment the whole thing was. Maybe I was spoiled when I was a kid because I was Pat Foster's son. Now, all of a sudden, I was just the water boy. And having Emery treat me awful the whole time didn't make it any easier. This was around the time that drag racing was becoming a big corporate thing with major sponsors. We had Schlitz and Old Milwaukee, and Don Prudhomme was with Pepsi. You couldn't even socialize with the kids on the other teams anymore. I believe that's still true now—there's hardly any mingling between teams, because they're afraid of giving away their secrets. It was strange that I couldn't talk to Snake's kid after the races anymore. Dad stayed at the shop while I was on the road, so he didn't see what was going on, but he could feel it.

It was especially sad because the *Blue Max* team were my heroes. Raymond Beadle was the driver, and he was a great guy. Waterbed Fred, a colorful guy in drag racing, was also there. But Emery—"Dale the Snail" they called him—treated me like garbage the whole time. They were three-time world champions, but when I got there, they weren't running worth a damn, and I'm sure Emery, as crew chief, was scrambling for answers. On top of that, my head wasn't in it 100 percent.

Dad just built a new car for them, and when we tested it, there were some problems. Emery immediately blamed Dad—he blamed everyone except himself. He had the car sonic tested because he didn't believe the chassis had the correct tubing thickness. The only thing that I saw wrong with the car was that the bar behind the seat where the shoulder harnesses were mounted was too high; when Raymond hit the throttle at the starting line, the Gs pushed his body up and his helmet hit the top of the roll cage. He was a great driver, he just couldn't see. One time I was standing on the starting line with Waterbed, who said right after the run, "You guys all witnessed that right? Raymond lost his balls right here and now." The crew jumped to conclusions about what was going on. Dad flew out and fixed the seatbelt, and the same car ended up winning drag racing's premier event at Indianapolis. The same car, the same tubing. Emery was just lost.

The final straw for me was an incident over a clutch cooler—a little exhaust fan that you use to cool down the clutch after a run so that you can work on it. The trailer had an outlet for the extension cords. The top one was 110 volts and the bottom was 220 volts, but they looked exactly alike. I plugged the fan in, but I put it into the 220 outlet by accident, and it was running super fast. It wasn't going to hurt anyone, but this was Emery's big chance: "You idiot! You're about the dumbest little jackass!" really giving it to me way more than I deserved. Dad was there, and I was embarrassed—it was like they were talking smack on him. I walked into Raymond's office and told him I was going back to California. When I left, it was one of the only times I ever saw my dad cry. I felt bad, too, mostly for him staying there with this guy. As time went on, everything got sorted out, but I still felt bad. I think Dad really wanted me to be with him. When I left, he knew I wasn't coming back. The whole thing was a bummer.

The *Blue Max* experience lasted six months. In Carmel, I moved back into my old place. I had left most of my belongings there, only taking what could fit in my car. Since I was never 100 percent sure that I'd stay in Dallas, I let one of my friends flop there. When I got back, the phone was disconnected—typical roommate B.S., running up a huge bill in my name. That messed me up with the phone company forever. In fact, I still don't have a phone in my name.

I got a job at a great little restaurant called The Wagon Wheel Coffee Shop. It was in a rural area of Carmel Valley, but it was a real famous place for big cowboy breakfasts. There was a two-hour wait to get in on weekends. Anyone who raced at Laguna Seca went there, and the Tubes stopped by to eat whenever they played in town. It was a kick-ass place and I made good money—I could pay the rent *and* put gas in the car. With the basics covered, I started goofing around more at Dave's body shop in Sand City. That's where I met a kid named Todd Gravelle and his younger brother, Chad. They worked part-time there, but their parents had a racecar-building shop in Salinas at the same complex I ended up in for years. It was also through Todd that I met Job Stevens, who is still one of my closest friends.

Cole takes a spin in his boat around Moss Landing Harbor with another instrumental early Salinas Boy, Todd Gravelle. *Cole & Susan Foster collection*

The Gravelle family has a long history of racing, mostly stock cars and sprint cars. After World War II, their grandpa owned midgets and dirt cars and was a good motor guy. Their father raced late-model stock cars on serious asphalt with guys like Dick Trickle. They were very successful on the West Coast, and they ran Dodges only (in fact, they had a dog named Mopar). Their dad was a very good fabricator and raced super modifieds, grandpa was the motor guy, and these two kids learned how to do everything. They were way beyond my friends and me—we were trying to figure out how to use a MIG welder and they could build an entire racecar.

When you're young, you've got all the time in the world, so we started to wrench. I still had a BMW, and Todd had one too. We were so wound up, we slammed them, put big sway bars on them, and shaved all the trim. We rebuilt the motors, fabricated skirts, and stuck spoilers on the front. I had a '76 with safety bumpers. The blinkers in the front stuck out, so I put in early-model signals and found they fit flush. I also put older bumpers on my late model—nice, smooth, round-blade types—and made them one piece by welding them together. Then we put the right wheels and tires on them. They were ahead of their time.

My first Beemer was an older one, a '68 2002. It got hit, but I received some insurance money and we were going to repaint the whole car. Dave Smith had it all prepped and ready, but I had a date and needed it for the weekend. I took it out and went to some parties, then dropped a girl off in Pebble Beach because I had another chick waiting at home. I was driving in the rain on a dark country road; the stereo was really loud, and I was listening to Bauhaus' "Bela Lugosi's Dead." All of a sudden, right in front of my headlights, there was a horse. I turned, but I nailed that thing head-on. Those BMW front fenders come to a sharp point in the front, and they're strong. That horse hit right above the headlight and the fender didn't even buckle, but the hood and the front apron were a mess. The impact pushed everything between the fenders a foot back into the radiator, and the hood came off the hinges and through the windshield.

So there I am in the middle of nowhere. The horse was breathing, lying there looking at me. I was looking at this horse, looking at my car, and all I could think was "Why did I take it out? It was primered, ready to paint, and now it's junk." Then that horse stood up right in front of the headlights and everything inside of it fell out on the road—intestines and who knows what else—with a big "plop." Everything was steaming, it was the sickest thing. Then, the thing started running around! Bauhaus was still playing and this horse was kicking and bouncing off fences and coming back toward me. I was thinking, "Die, dammit! Die!" Finally, it went toes up like a cartoon. A car came around the corner and swerved around me and ran right through the blood. The next car was a sheriff's car. I had smoked a joint earlier that night, but I wasn't messed up, just a little paranoid. The cops were supercool. They said, "You're lucky. We just had an officer die hitting a deer."

Not too many people had horses around there, and it ended up belonging to a local family that owned a tree service and seemed to be doing well. They tried to deny responsibility, but I still got five hundred bucks out of them. I got lucky and found another 2002. I took Dad with me to look at it. It was a real clean car, but they told me the motor was blown. We lifted the hood, and it was knocking, but Dad noticed it was just a loose bracket. He said, "Yeah, it's kind of bad. I'll give you eight hundred for it." We took it, tightened up the bracket, and it was perfect.

I was living in Carmel while Clint Eastwood was mayor. In fact, I dated his daughter Allison. I also started going out to Salinas to work at the Gravelles' shop quite a bit. For a couple of years, we took over the shop at night after Grandma and Grandpa went home. We did paint jobs on the side. Grandma and Grandpa hated us because Todd and Chad were "good kids." Not that Job and I corrupted them exactly—they were still good kids. They only knew racing and the shop, so we took them out into the real world, introduced them to girls and parties, and the grandparents lost their death grip on them. But they taught us a ton, and having free reign of their shop was great. That's when I really made the decision that I wasn't going into racecars. What happened in Texas was miserable, but it gave me a taste of that life and I'm glad I got it out of my system. If I hadn't gone, I might still be jonesing, not knowing what it would've been like. Now I'm 100 percent certain that I made the right decision.

I started going to Salinas because the Gravelle brothers had a shop with mills, lathes, welders—everything you need to build a racecar. I went out there a lot with Job, one of my best friends. He was a surfer kid from Pacific Grove who had a Volkswagen bus. We were just poor kids who needed a place to work on cars, and this was it. Job was younger than me and from a different scene, but we were both fairly popular, and I think the Gravelle brothers were just stoked to have us around.

Back then, if you hung out in Salinas, you were aware of Buck and George Thomas, two brothers who were the kings of the weekend cruise. Buck had a '34 Ford three-window and George had a '33 Plymouth with a license plate that read "Red N Wet." I was impressed with their cars, but at first they were not very impressed with us. They were probably ten years older than us, which would have put them in their early thirties, but they never told us how old they were. They were mysterious like that.

George was a union ironworker, and Buck did hot rods and bodywork out of their shops, which they lived at right there on Burton Avenue, where Rod Powell still is and where I was for almost twenty years. Buck and George were hillbillies who came down from Oregon, and were originators of the live-at-your-shop lifestyle. They really had their places fixed up—fully badass apartments. One even had a chandelier.

Buck is a real good body guy, real meticulous, using a torch and hammer welding. After we started hanging around, he taught us a ton of good basics, but he never said, "Good job, guys"; it was more like, "You guys are wusses. I'm the king, and you guys can't do jack." As we got better, it became a little competitive. When I do anything, I always want to do it well. Maybe he saw me as some sort of threat. But he was talented and smart with a good sense of humor, and he liked hanging out with us. He liked the girls we ran with and got in on the action a little bit.

Buck just hated the police and tormented them whenever he could. He was like a jailhouse lawyer. Whenever he got pulled over, he knew just what to say to push the cops as far as he could without ending up on the ground. Those guys were classic in a lot of ways. They had a famous rule about never letting a guy ride in the car with them. It was girls only, and I don't think they ever broke the rule. If you were lying on the street with a broken leg, there was no way you would get a ride to the hospital unless you were a chick.

Buck also acted like he didn't care about magazines. If anyone wanted to shoot his car he'd say, "I don't want you to," but he really did. George was always up for fun, while Buck was a little too negative.

Buck and George teased us a lot about our cars. They didn't think BMWs were cool, but they knew we had 2002s because that's what we could afford. Looking back, all that teasing and calling us queers pushed us to do what we had to do to get into customs. After a few months of hanging around, I bought a '55 Chevy from a GI in Monterey, Job bought a '50 Ford, Chad bought a '57 Dodge Coronet, and Todd got a '53 Chevy. We all started building them at the same time. Then Buck sold his coupe and bought a '50 Plymouth, and Chad got a '50 Merc, so we were all doing customs.

I was still living in the Carmel Valley and going to Salinas to work on cars, so I realized that I needed my own shop. I had a friend named Eric Stein who was an artist and never really worked, but always had money (maybe it came from his parents). We became friends, and he saw that I was passionate about cars, and he wanted to help out. One day he asked, "What would you think about getting a shop?" I told him that would be great but that I had no money. So he asked, "Well, what would it take?" The only available place I knew of was where Chad and the rest of those guys were in Salinas, so I went and checked it out. I didn't have credit, but Eric had the money for the first and last months' rent, plus the deposit. We rented the shop, and he bought me a MIG welder, a chop saw, and some basic die grinders. Until then, I was just another guy with a set of hand tools, but now I had a shop, thanks to Eric.

Top: Cole and George Thomas liberate a go-kart engine. George and his brother Buck, Cole recalls, were "the kings of the weekend cruise" in Salinas and provided important feedback— positive and negative—in the formation of Salinas Boys. *Cole & Susan Foster collection*

Middle: A seminal supporter of the early Salinas Boys, hot rod paint legend Rod Powell. *Cole & Susan Foster collection*

Bottom: With Eric Stein, one of Cole's early patrons. "I did stuff for Eric whenever I could, but he never asked for a dime back." *Cole & Susan Foster collection*

I helped Eric whenever I could, not that he ever asked for a dime back. He spent about ten grand—a lot of money twenty years ago. He did something for me that my parents never could do, and it was unconditional. There were times when he wasn't doing as well and he'd stay at the shop with me, but he was a very sweet guy who never held anything over my head, never once said, "Hey, you owe me." With someone like that, you always think there are going to be strings attached, but with Eric there never were, and that's rare in life. He really was an enabler; he helped out other people too. He passed away in 2006, only in his fifties. He recognized my skills early on, and I don't think I would've ever done this without him.

Eric always helped me pay the rent if I was short, and I was short about half the time. I still worked at restaurants and catered at banquets, whatever I could do for money. It was hard to make the crossover to cars full time, and besides, there was still a lot to learn. The little bit of money the shop made was from spot jobs. Kids would crash their Hondas or Rabbits, so you'd tell them, "Go get the insurance money, and I'll split it with you." We never had too many complaints. When your only work comes from word of mouth, you've got to make everyone happy. If you screw one person over, that's the end of it. Sometimes we'd mess up, so we'd eat it on the money, which is part of the learning process.

After doing these small jobs, we got better, and we wanted to chop Job's '50 Ford. We sort of went around Buck and asked Butch Hurlhey how to do it. Butch was an easygoing older guy who had been doing bodywork since the 1950s. He worked as Rod Powell's metal guy for ten or fifteen years, and he gave us some confidence: "You guys can do this. I'll come check on you." We hid the car at my place and did it over the weekend. When Buck saw it, he just walked up and said, "You guys ruined it." We hadn't, of course, but Buck just took over. Poor Job was caught in the middle. At any rate, when it was done, it was done right. With Buck, everything had to be super-clean—no shortcuts. It was all the way or nothing. He'd always say, "We're not just going through the motions here, boys." We learned a good work ethic, which is the foundation for how I work today.

When we started my '55 Chevy we went around Buck again. Chad and I thought, "We can do it." Once again we talked to Butch for confidence. "You start it,

and the car will tell you what to do," he told us. "If you remove these pieces of the puzzle, you'll know where to put those pieces back." We did it simply. It had Weld wheels when they first came out. It looked like a Super Gas car. I mean, it was slammed. I couldn't get the rear tires out without taking the rearend out of the car, but it still had a backseat. It had a four-speed and a 350, and was a good-running car. We put a Ford nine-inch in it and swapped the frame rails to put the stock leaf springs to the inside—a simple way to tub it. We put stock-car springs in the front, and the bumpers were welded together. The bird and door handles were shaved, the headlight rings were painted, and it was smooth. It was '80s for sure, but it looked good.

By 1986, we had our own style of paint. Job painted his '50 Ford a sort of purple-magenta, while Buck did a '50 Plymouth in a flat aqua color. When we first had them all done, we took them to a show in Merced. It was weird to look around and realize that our cars were some of the nicest there. The colors were popular and people asked, "What are these?" and took pictures. We really B.S.'d people about how we did them. Buck insisted that we didn't tell anyone, which was probably smart. We made up stories that we put powdered something or another in the primer. I remember telling that to Rod Powell, but he probably didn't buy it.

Job's '50 Ford at the 1987 Paso Robles show. *Cole & Susan Foster collection*

Left: Cole's '55 Chevy, 1986. Cole bought the car from a GI in Monterey after giving up Bimmers. *Cole & Susan Foster collection*

Right: Todd Gravelle's '53 Chevy. "By 1986, we had our own style of paint," Cole says. "We really B.S.'d people about how we did them. Buck insisted that we didn't tell anyone. We made up stories that we put powdered something or another in the primer." *Cole & Susan Foster collection*

We also took our first trip to Paso Robles in 1986, the four of us in that '55 Chevy—Job, Buck, Chad, and me. There were these badass Mexican guys there who were maybe a year or two older than me. They had a little yellow coupe and tattoos, and were playing crazy rockabilly. We were intimidated by them, they were so badass. It was Rudy Rodriguez.

I also remember seeing a high school–age kid sitting in the grass drawing. He liked Job's '50 Ford and drew a picture of it, then gave it to him. That was Keith Weesner. Back then it was really a graybeard deal, all these old guys who didn't really know what to make of us. You could count the young guys on one hand. When we got back, I started building my '54 Chevy.

I sold the '55 Chevy to this guy named Freddy who was from the San Fernando Valley. Earlier, he paid $25,000 for Buck's coupe, which was almost unheard of back then. That was when I first met him; he was in Salinas while I was building my '55. He just walked into my shop, this little fast-talking guy, saw a poster of my dad's car on the wall, and said, "Pat Foster, good friend of mine. Whose '55? Call me when it's done. I'll buy it," then he was gone. Who was this guy that brought a suitcase full of money for Buck?

I ended up selling the '55 to him about a year later. I called him, and he said, "OK, I'll be there tomorrow." He drove up from L.A. and said, "Take me around the block.

Don't scare me, just let me hear it run." At the time I had a bunch of unpaid tickets, but I took him around the block anyway and, sure enough, I got pulled over by the highway patrol. I told him, "I have a warrant, Fred. I'm going to jail."

I told him to take the car back to the shop and give the guys the money, and that I'd talk to him later. The cop ran my deal and said, "Get out of the car, you're going to jail." I asked if it was OK if my "uncle" took the car, and the cop said, "No way. It's going on the tow truck." I was polite, but the cop was a prick. He took me in, and I called the boys at the shop from jail and said, "Hey, did Freddy leave the money? My car is impounded, and I have to pay to get it out." They said, "No, he didn't leave anything, man. He just split." Eric had to come get me out of jail.

So now I have a big fine, I have to go to court, *and* my car's been impounded. I really needed money and was mad at Freddy for not helping me out of a jam. I called him after I got the car back, and he said to bring it down. Buck had a car he was going to try to sell at the Pomona swap meet, so I thought, "Hell, I'll sell mine there too." I knew I had it sold to Freddy for eight grand, but since he didn't give me a deposit, if I could sell it at the swap meet for ten, I'd sell it. We drove down to Pomona and tubbed cars were in. Mine looked and sounded good, but it wasn't getting much action, so I started it up, hopped it

Cole's '55 and Buck's Plymouth at Carmel Beach. Cole later sold the car to a key grip named Freddy and it ended up on an episode of *Beverly Hills 90210* with a Pro Stock hood and new paint. *Cole & Susan Foster collection*

A pen-and-ink Cole did for his dad, 1986. Cole recalls attending a seminar in downtown L.A. for promising young high school artists: "All I did was draw a Funny Car!" *Pat Foster collection*

around the parking lot, and chirped it. I got a big crowd around it and all kinds of action. Kids were crying, begging their dads to buy it for them, and suddenly I had a bidding war going on. I was thinking, "I'm going to do really good," when the likeable little tyrant Freddy came busting through the people, yelling, "Get away from my car! What are you doing, kid? That's my car you're selling!" Before I could say anything, he was already half-hustling the deal and took over the bidding. I took the money, and Freddy took the car.

The story doesn't end there though, because the car ended up starring in an episode of *Beverly Hills 90210.* Freddy worked in television as a grip, and they saw the car at the studio. He called and said, "Hey, your old car is going to be on *90210.*" He had put a big Pro Stock hood on it and painted it shiny green. They were doing an episode where Steve, the blond guy, gets into a drag race with a Chevy II or something. It was a big deal in Salinas. My girlfriend got all her friends together, and we all watched it. At one point, they lifted the hood, and I said, "That was my motor." Freddy said that he got as much for that shoot as he had paid me for it, but I wasn't mad because it wasn't the greatest car in the world when I sold it. Freddy finished it—real paint, fully upholstered—in fact, it was later in *Hot Rod.* I still see Freddy every now and again.

By then I was building my '54 Chevy. You have to remember that back then there were no automotive TV shows, no Internet, no nothing, really, so it was hard to learn. Plus we had to deal with Buck, and as far as we knew, he was the best on the planet. That's what he told us, anyway. He has a great eye and was quick to point out mistakes on other people's cars. We'd get a new car magazine and it was like school. He would say, "Now what did that guy do wrong?" It was always negative. We were taught to be picky. If it wasn't right, we'd say so. It was just like with Schwinn Sting-rays back in the Valley.

My friends and I went to parties after high school because there was nothing else to do in Monterey. One night we were out in my '55, and there was trouble with some guys from another town who almost ran over some girls. About five cars took off after this Jeep full of guys.

Left: The Foster boys, 1988: Pat, J. T., Dan, and Cole. *Cole & Susan Foster collection*

Other cars started dropping out, but the '55 was running strong. The guy would run red lights, but we were on him the whole way. They pulled up at this liquor store in the town of Seaside and everyone jumped out. One kid ran into the liquor store, another took off into the neighborhood, and one guy sat around a little bit and took some licks. The kid who ran into the liquor store came out with a big stick and dropped Todd. Noah and I chased him back in, and the kid ran behind the counter.

We were taking out gum racks and coffee pots, anything that was in our way, trying to get to this kid, when an old man popped up swinging a bat and split my nose wide open. I was thinking, "It's probably time to go." Outside, Todd and Chad were bending back every door on the Jeep. Job was the only smart one—he never got out of the car.

I lit up my car, and the guys jumped in, and as we were pulling out, these huge Gallo wine jugs started hitting the car. I backed up about fifteen feet, put it to the floor, and caved in the whole side of that Jeep, pushing it onto the sidewalk. Broken glass, broken nose, wasted car, gang fight—we all knew we were in trouble.

We split, and I told Chad to put my car in the garage out in Salinas. Then I went to the emergency room because I wouldn't stop bleeding. I gave them a fake name, and they stitched me up. I didn't want to put myself at the scene, in case a police report came over the radio. I told them I was breaking up a fight at a party and took a stray hit. The doctor said, "Well, if there was any violence, we have to call the police." I said I'd be happy to talk to them and that I was going to go outside and get some fresh air. Then I just ran.

Back at the shop Buck said, in his jailhouse lawyer talk, "Well, whenever something like this happens, the first one to call the cops usually wins." So we all got our stories together and went down to the Seaside Police Department. They said, "We've been looking for you guys—you're in a lot of trouble. Just sit tight." Half an hour went by and Buck, who was with us, said, "To hell with these guys. You're not under arrest. Let's go."

The next day we all hustled to fix my car and make it look like it never happened. We also came up with a plan. Chad and Todd told our story to their grandfather, who was a judge in Monterey—how we were trying to catch these guys. I didn't even remember what the truth

was anymore, but the police called us not long after. This time they treated us like we had been given the key to the city: "Hello, fellows. I'm glad you could make it. Would you like some coffee?" We gave our statement and never heard another word about it.

I knew it was time to grow up. I'm not going to get brain damage defending some chicks I don't even know. My nasal cavity is still messed up. I learned the hard way not to be a hero—it usually doesn't pay off.

The original Salinas Boys: Todd Gravelle, Job Stevens, and Cole. *Cole & Susan Foster collection*

Chad Gravelle, Job, and Cole. *Cole & Susan Foster collection*

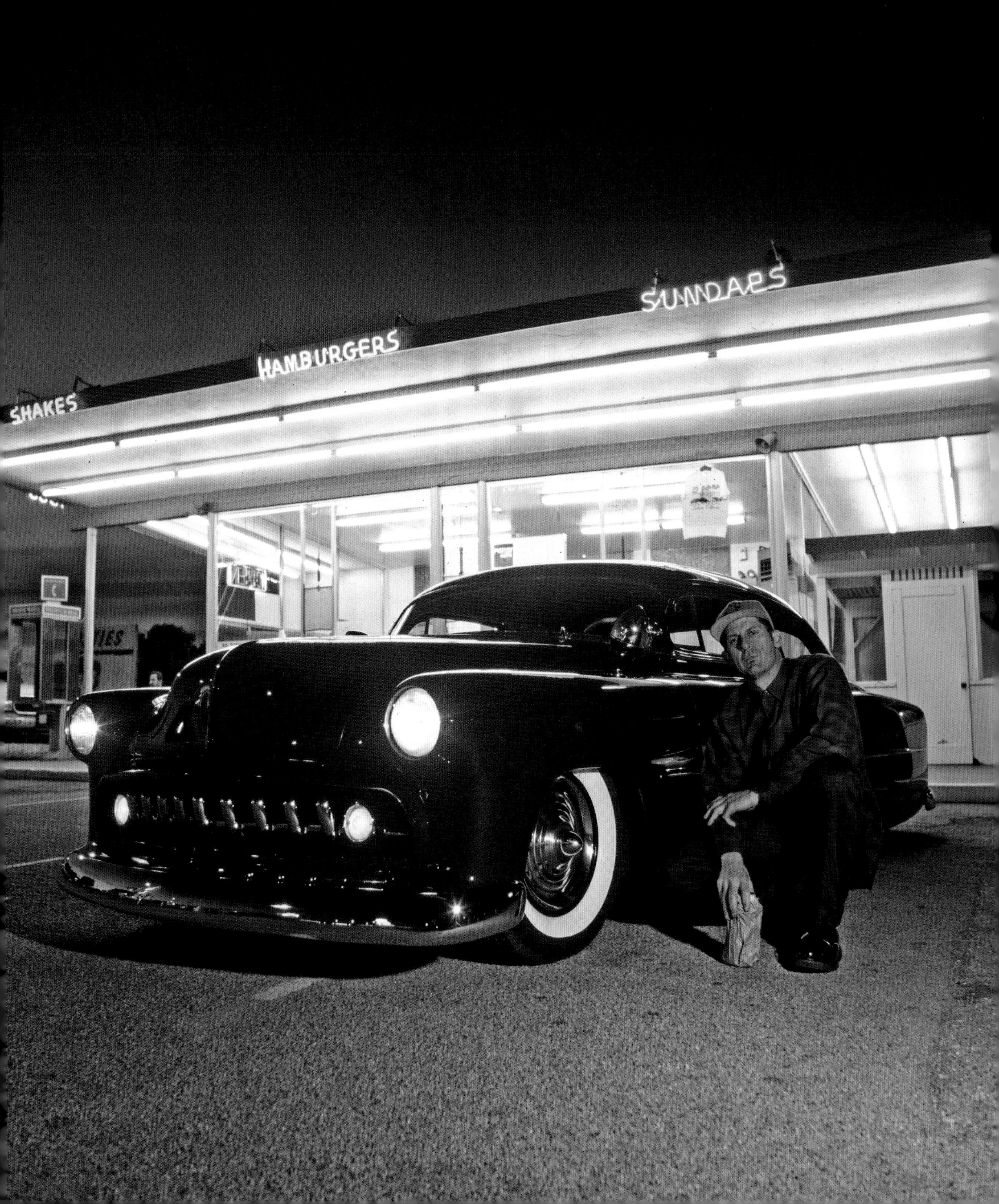
SHAKES
HAMBURGERS
SUNDAES

CHAPTER THREE

CUSTOMS BECOME KING

I started building customs because I could buy a car for five hundred dollars. I already had a garage to work in, so I didn't need much money—it was pure time and labor, like when I was a kid doing bicycles. When BMX came in, I couldn't afford it, so I just did my own thing.

Chad and Todd's dad's shop had moved ten miles away, so they were coming over more often, and Job worked on his car out of my shop. We were all doing our own things and helping each other, but trying to outdo each other at the same time. Chad redid his '57 Dodge, going off in a different direction by putting a bunch of his dad's NASCAR parts on it, like a quick-change rearend and full roll cage. Later, he got a '50 Merc that he started

The Salinas Boys name started as a lark, playing off the Dogtown and Z Boys skate team and featuring the "z" that still sticks in some quarters. Today the name is accompanied by a variety of decidedly more stylish Keith Weesner renderings. *Cole & Susan Foster collection*

doing traditional, but he inherited some money from his grandma and went really high-tech. We were competitive, and people started to take notice of what we were doing.

After the show in Merced, *Custom Rodder* came to my shop and did a piece on us. Young guys building cars was very much a novelty back then. They called us "the Salinas Kids," which pissed us off because we were the Salinas Boys, damn it. The whole Salinas Boyz thing began as a joke when we went to Paso Robles that first time. On the entry form it asked for your club's name, so we put down Salinas Boyz with a "z" like the Dog Town skaters, the "Z Boys." I drew it on the shop wall with a skull and two crossed pistons, something like the Zephyr Skate team would've done.

When we first heard about the *Custom Rodder* article, Buck was against them coming. He wanted to stay underground. He ended up being in the pictures, but wanted his number left out of it. They put my number in there, and he was pissed about that, too. But there it was, the first few pages of ink we ever got, and it called us the Salinas Kids. The freelance writer, Dave Hill, would always mess up my name.

"Cole Porter, right?"

"No, Foster."

"The Salinas Kids, right?"

"No, it's Boys."

Despite the article, the Salinas Boyz name stuck. None of us were much older than twenty-one; in fact, Job was eighteen. After I put that early Salinas Boys logo on the wall, I decided I wanted an official logo for us, so I asked Keith Weesner to come up with something. I'd see him every year at Paso, and I'd hit him up for a logo. I'd say, "I want an old-time Pep Boys kind of logo," but he was very shy. I kept pressing him, and finally he took out a little yellow Post-it and showed me what he had in mind. I took it home, cleaned it up, and printed it. I still have that logo on my website—I mean, the kid was that good. He later came up with the shirt with my Chevy on it, which we gave out at the show to our friends. I still sell that shirt on my website.

It's always been a loose thing, the Salinas Boys name. I think some people might have thought it was a super custom factory, when really it was just a bunch of guys doing their thing in this little shop. But going to car shows attracted other people, and we started doing their cars.

I wasn't waiting or bussing tables anymore. I was at the shop all the time, sleeping on the couch and barely making it. I worked on other peoples' cars during the day and on my '54 at night.

Eric still helped with money sometimes, because the shop rent just barely got paid. Then I got my first big customer. The job came through a local guy I knew named Greg Lazerini. He was doing cars himself, hot rods mostly, but decided he was just going to work on his dad's farm. He had this '48 Cadillac fastback that belonged to Jerry Wilkinson, who owned a company that built all the freeways around here. He made some really good money and retired at forty. So he had this two-door '48 Cadillac with a cherry body, and Greg gave me the outline of what he was going to do. We just took over the job, putting in a 500-inch Cadillac motor with a Turbo 400 and a Caddy rearend. Then I figured out that a Camaro clip would fit in the front and from there took the car the whole way to completion. It had a mohair interior, and I put power windows in it, since I had a good basic knowledge of electronics. It had a modern drivetrain but from the outside it looked pure 1940s. We rented a booth and painted it ourselves, too. It was my first full-on restoration.

When Jerry first saw it, he said, "Goddamn it, I think that thing is too low." That Camaro clip really lowered it, but it looked good. Jerry had a house in Palm Springs, so he took it to a show down there, and it won Best of

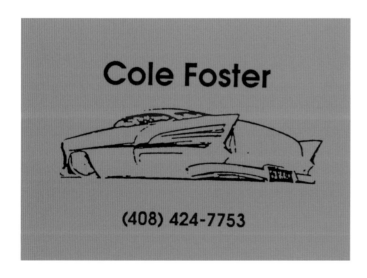

Cole Foster

(408) 424-7753

First business card. *Cole & Susan Foster collection*

Show. Everyone told him how bitchin' it sat, so after that he trusted me and brought me another Cadillac, a '59 convertible, and said, "Whatever you did to that one, do it to this one." It was just a restoration, but it was perfect enough to paint black, and after it was lowered, it looked really cool. We charged by the hour—time and materials—the same as now. I think we did that whole Cadillac for $25,000, including paint. That was a lot of money for us back then, but it took about a year to do the car.

THE BLUE '54

A year could easily go by, between doing a big job like that, hustling girls, and trying to work on my '54 Chevy. I always found time to do it, because I wanted a custom so badly. My favorite thing about a custom was that you could do all the work yourself—it was all labor for the most part. You could be the richest guy in the world and still have the ugliest custom. Money can make a car win at the drag strip, but it doesn't make a custom beautiful, and that was what I liked about it, because I certainly didn't have any money. It wasn't about building the quickest car in town, either. It was all about your eye and proving that you could do the work. I think I've always had the eye; I just had to catch up with being able to pull it off technically.

After the two Cadillacs, I was doing spot paint jobs and whatever I could to scrounge up a few dollars. My girlfriend at the time went to school in San Francisco, so she was gone five days a week and came back on the weekends. So on those five nights, I would hit the '54 hard, pulling late-nighters on it. The guys were helping out quite a bit. Job, Todd, Chad, and even Buck helped me with that car at first. The first thing I did was change out the motor; the one I still have in it came from a friend's Nova, a 350.

I learned a lot with that car. I put drop spindles on it at first, but I broke them a couple of times and ended up putting a Mustang II suspension kit under it and changing out the rearend. I didn't take the body off of it, but did a nice engine compartment. After that, I cut the roof and drove it for a while. The '54 was the first car I chopped myself. I remember looking at a lot of different chops before I did it, most of which showed me what not to do. When I cut the '54, I just tried to use my own judgment and personal tastes.

Two rare shots of the "blue" '54, one with Cole-applied flames in 1992 and another in its Jesse Cruz–mixed purple. "It's a shame that not too many people ever saw it" in purple, Cole says, "because it was just beautiful." The pearl mix would influence his choice of paint for the red shop truck. *Cole & Susan Foster collection*

When I had some money saved, I could take a week off and just work on it. It was the only car I had, so I did it in sections. I'd usually set a goal, like "I'm going to yank the motor out and do the whole engine compartment" or "I'm going to do the taillights and back half." Doing it that way, the car took a few years to finish.

Back on the '55 we had started messing around with flat paint, so when I had the '54 squared away my friend Jesse Cruz painted the car with pearl-base paint. When he based it, he only had slow reducer. It looked so iridescent without the clear on it that he said, "I think it would really look cool if we did something like this." So I kind of got credited with the first modern satin job, but Jesse was right there. We mixed some blue and purple, and he knew how to lay on a super-smooth base coat without dry spots. It was spectacular.

I took it to the first Hot Rod Reunion in Bakersfield, and it just killed them. People really freaked out on that color. It got a little bit of coverage that day, but I really wasn't getting any customers like I thought I would, so I decided that it needed to be in finished paint for people to think I was really good. It didn't have glass in it, and the interior and the chrome weren't done. I can't believe I did it now, but in one month I made glass for it, painted it, and did the interior, just in time to take it to the Oakland Roadster Show. I was exhausted just driving to that thing, but I was also really excited. It was a romantic

thing for me to go to that show. I had heard about it when I lived in L.A., and I remembered my dad going.

Since I'd never really entered a show before, I asked Rod Powell who I should talk to when I got there. He told me that the guy running the show was Rick Perry, and to tell him that "Rod sent me" and he'd set me up. The day we left, it was pouring rain, so I tried to get a trailer, but I couldn't, so I just towed it, and it poured the whole way. When we got to the Oakland Coliseum, it was just miserable, with wind howling through the place, and the car had mud on the side. I asked around and finally found Perry. He was talking to some people, so I patiently waited until he was done. When he finally got free, I said, "Hi, Mr. Perry. My name's Cole Foster. Rod Powell sent me. Maybe you could tell me what I need to do." He looked at me and said, "I don't care who you are. I don't have time for you. Get out of my face." I just about dropped tears. I mean, I was so stoked to be there and it was a miracle that the car was even done in time, and in one sentence he just crushed me. I told the guys, "To hell with this. Let's go home." But they talked me into staying.

Right: The business end of the famous blue '54. Cole reshaped the grille opening and replaced the parking-light pods with four extra teeth, then lowered the stock bumper. The headlights are frenched with '54 Merc rings. *Jesus Espinoza, DeadendMagazine.com*

Above: "I had a picture in my head of what it was going to look like, and it came out exactly like I thought it would." That mind's-eye picture of the blue '54 included chopping the top four inches and replacing the rear of the roof with custom-rolled sheet metal from Don Fretwell, thus eliminating the factory rear pillar and resulting in the tapered slope. The Chevy's wraparound rear window was replaced with smaller glass from a 1950 Plymouth. The car was the first to bring national attention to Cole and the Salinas Boys. *Bo Bertilsson*

Above: The white tuck-and-roll inside the '54 features blue piping—tasteful and effective. The speedo's factory, but the rest of the gauges are aftermarket, nestled into an engine-turned panel. The wheel comes from a 1953 Merc. *Bo Bertilsson*

Left: The blue '54's hubcaps are 1951 DeSoto with modified bullet centers. *Bo Bertilsson*

The blue '54 features a 350 Chevy from a friend's Nova mated to a Turbo 350 tranny. Cole pulled a lot of all-nighters finishing the car. Other major installations included a Mustang II IFS and a '64 Chevy axle out back. *Bo Bertilsson*

So I put the '54 Chevy in the show. We went and bought rock salt to put around it, and it looked good. But it came in absolutely dead last because I didn't want to open anything up, and I still stick to that. I left the doors shut and the hood closed because a custom is all about the lines, and when you open it up it breaks them, it just kills a custom. It's not like a hot rod where you can have the hood on or off. But even though this car was totally nice underneath the hood, I just couldn't stand to break the line, so I left her closed. The window was down so that you could look in it, but the judges wanted the doors open and the trunk popped.

I spent a lot of time thinking about that car before I did it. I had a picture in my head of what it was going to look like, and it came out exactly like I thought it would. When I finish a build, I don't have a bunch of "would have, could have, should haves." I think about those things beforehand. I still love the '54. It's like a good old friend that I take out once in a while, give it some loving. It's not perfect anymore—not that it ever was—but it inspired a lot of other '54 Chevys around the world, and I think it stands up to every one of them.

ROCKIN' 'N' ROLLIN'

When Job, the boys, and I first starting going to car shows in 1986 or 1987, we were the only young guys there, but by the early 1990s, other guys our age started showing up: the Chislers, the Shifters, the Lucky Devils, the Beatniks wearing their purple shirts—all of that started right around then. I didn't think being in a club was good for business. It was like a conflict of interest. Besides, we had our own deal going. I didn't need tattoos and I didn't need a jacket. Out of all the clubs, the one that I was good friends with was the Lonely Kings. The Kennedy brothers were in the Lonely Kings, along with my friends Chris Prokopow, Gary Fry, Derek Coon, Kutty Noteboom, and Rico Fodrey. I got to know Mike Ness through the Lonely Kings.

Of course, I'd seen Social Distortion ten years earlier, in 1982, and thought they were great. Then I'd see Mike pop up at car shows every once in a while, and I continued to see his band from time to time. Around 1984, we went to one of his shows in Chad's '57 Dodge, a slammed black car with a silver roof. Mike spent some time checking it out. A few more years went by, and there he was walking around my '54 Chevy at Paso with a Lonely Kings jacket on. He started asking a lot of questions because he had a '53 Chevy that he was thinking about doing. He was very pleasant and very humble.

Later, he started talking to me about working on his '55 Pontiac. Soon after, he called to say that he was coming up to Santa Cruz to play, and that he'd drive his Pontiac up. He dropped the car off at my shop and would come and work on it when he had some time off. He'd stay for a couple of days and then go on tour, and when the tour was over, they'd drop him off in Salinas. As a musician he was one of my heroes. We started going through the car, and he had a childlike enthusiasm about it. Before he

Above: The '54 earns some hardware at Paso, 1992. The award is being presented by renowned automotive artist Steve Stanford. *Cole & Susan Foster collection*

Right: Ness stops in to check the progress on the Pontiac. Cole says, "He had a childlike enthusiasm about it. He'd push me to be a little more radical, and I'd calm him back down." *Cole & Susan Foster collection*

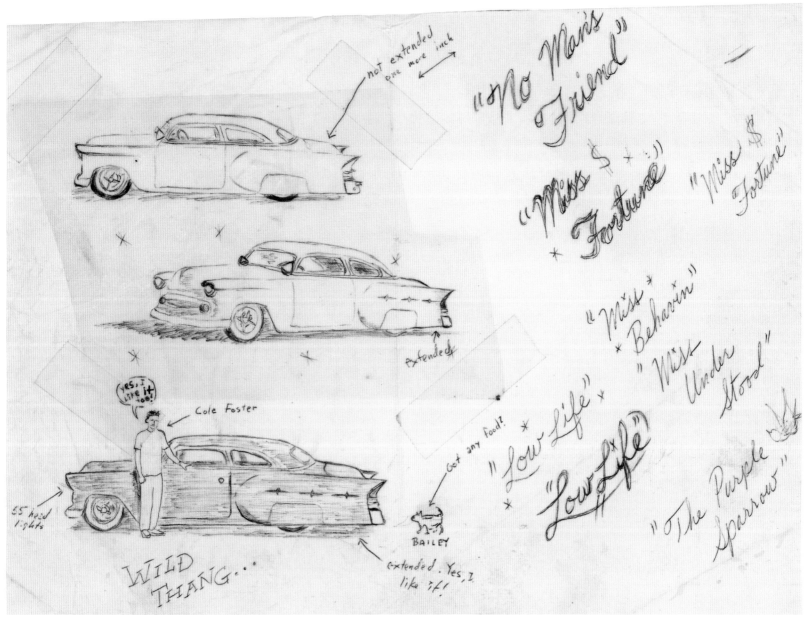

This page and next: Cole and Mike Ness traded concept drawings during work on the Pontiac and the '54 Chevy that followed. Those are Ness' comments in cursive handwriting, Cole's in the printed hand. *Cole & Susan Foster collection*

brought the car in, he did drawings that he thought looked good, and then I would comment on them, but we usually found a happy medium. He'd push me to be a little more radical, and I'd calm him back down.

When Mike took the car home, it was all in black primer, but later he ended up doing a secondary color on it, a purple satin. We went to one of those Hootenanny rock/car shows a year after that, and here comes this car, a purple '55 Pontiac, and it has the '54 grille Job and I put on it. Those cars really don't have a grille opening,

so we made one and changed the bumper. We did some radical stuff to that frontend and of course figured this had to be Ness' car. So we started looking at the car, and I thought, "God, this looks screwed up. We did a crappy job on this thing." Then I realized that some kid had cloned the car, and it was just a little bit off. It was weird to see it plagiarized so perfectly and so quickly. Later, when I saw Ness backstage, I said, "Man, we saw this car . . ." and he said, "Yeah, that kid's been cruising by my house every day haunting me."

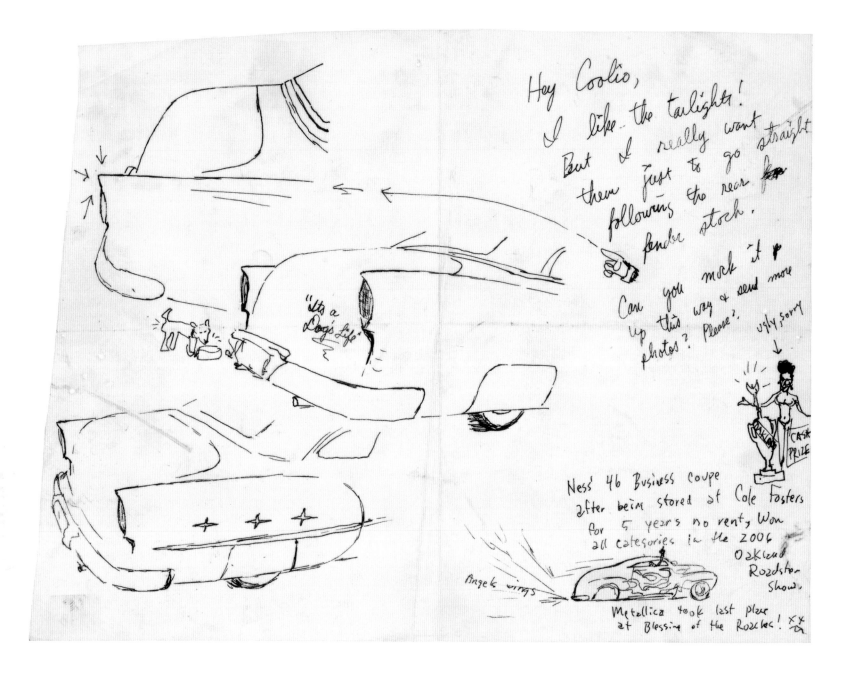

After that we worked on Mike's '54 Chevy. He had some local guy in Orange County work on it a bit and had a six-cylinder built for it. He wanted the roof done next and brought it up to our place. It was there for a year or so. He'd send money when he could, and we went through that car. A kid named Corey Conyers and I cut the roof. Corey was a talented kid from Kansas who worked under my dad for a couple of years and wanted to come out to California. He ended up staying for about three years. The first thing we did together was chop Mike's car.

At that point, the taillights weren't frenched; it was just in black satin. It said something silly on the back, like "Hoodoo Voodoo" or something. Then the motor blew up, and Mike brought the car back up to me. We went through the suspension and put a 327 he was building in it for him, and I finished up a few details, changed the drip rails on the top, and got it ready for paint. That car is super nice. There's a picture of him with it on the back of one of his album sleeves. It has real bitchin' dark candy-red paint job by my friend Marcos Garcia at Lucky Seven in Antioch.

continued on page 47

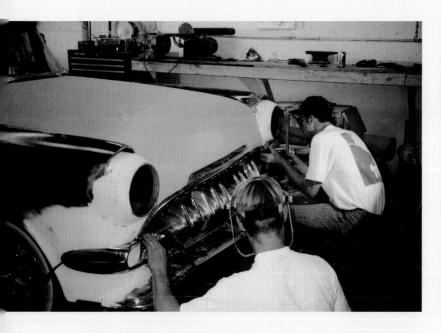

Job and Cole fit a '54 grille into the reworked opening of Mike Ness' '55 Pontiac, circa 1992–1993. *Cole & Susan Foster collection*

With Mike Ibbetson and Ness' '55 Pontiac. *Cole & Susan Foster collection*

Anybody can build a car. It takes a real man to cut one apart. Corey Conyers gets down to business on Ness' '54. *Cole & Susan Foster collection*

Corey and Cole on the Ness '54. *Cole & Susan Foster collection*

Next spread: Cole and Corey Conyers chopped Mike Ness' '54, and the Salinas Boys went over the suspension and installed a 327 for Mike. Marcos Garcia at Lucky Seven in Antioch sprayed the red paint. *David Perry*

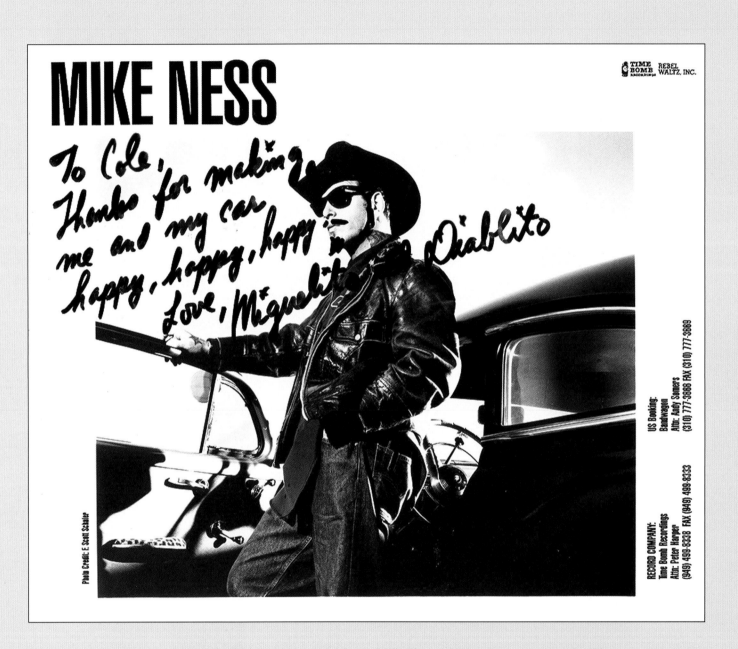

This is the big time, baby . . . this is rock 'n' roll. A Mike Ness publicity photo, costarring the '54.
Time Bomb Recordings photo by F. Scott Schafer

continued from page 42

Billy Gibbons, on the other hand, I met in a totally random fashion. Shortly after a picture of my shop truck was in *Custom Rodder*, I came into the shop one day, and one of the boys said, "Hey, there's some weird message on the machine from Billy F Gibbons." I said, "I think that's the guy from ZZ Top. Why would he be calling?" We definitely thought it was a crank call, because I had had no contact with him before that. So we played the message at least ten times. I gave the number a call and, sure enough, it was Billy on his tour bus heading somewhere. He complimented me on the truck and told me that Dusty Hill, ZZ Top's bass player, loved it, too.

We were on the phone for hours. It went from compliments to him asking me a few questions to him talking about a car that maybe I could do for him. I was flattered to death. Then the next night, he called my house at like 11 p.m. "This is Billy. What's happening?" and we would talk again. It was a trip, man. Once, he called me from the place of the guy who makes his amps and said, "Check this out," then played a couple of riffs. Crazy. So we went steady like this for a long time, and he got more serious about doing a car along the way. He came up with the old Chevy logo, and it was going to be the "OK Chevrolet." He sent me pictures of a sedan he had in his warehouse, and I did renderings. I thought it was a go.

He also sent me a lot of interesting things in the mail. One of the letters came from Tupelo, Mississippi, and had some blades of grass and a hundred-dollar bill in it. The letter said "Here's some Mississippi honey grass from the King's birthplace and a 100-dollar bill from the Mississippi bank, celebrating our new adventure with the OK Chevrolet." So, it was on—the hundred-dollar bill was our handshake.

Around Christmastime, Billy said, "Let's get past the holidays. Call me right after New Year's, and I'll get the car shipped out." I mean, this was it—I finally made it. On January 1, I wanted to call him so bad, but I thought I'll wait until January 4 or so. When I did call, I said, "Billy said to call him on the first," and Denise, the girl at his office, got really literal on me. "Really? He wanted you to call him on New Year's Day?" I just never got a call back, and I didn't understand it. How could he be so excited about it and then nothing?

About a year went by, and I got really depressed over it. When the deal was on, I told my whole family. "We're doing a car for Billy Gibbons, and it'll be the baddest thing ever," but it just never happened. I don't think it was because of something I did. I just think he got caught up making an album. He focuses hard on one thing at a time—the same as Ness—and when they change channels, if you're not walking right next to them, then you're not on that channel. So a year went by, and Billy called me that next year on New Year's Day, which was weird. He said, "I was thinking about you, so I thought I'd give you a New Year's Day call." I asked him what he was up to, and he said, "I'm playing the inauguration later this month." I said, "Well, that's more than I'm doing." He said, "I might not agree with Bush, but when the president calls and asks you to play his inauguration, you don't say no." He brought up the car a little bit, but by then, I just wanted to end it. I didn't want our relationship to be awkward, so I said, "Let's just be friends and not let this car thing come between us." I'd still like to do something for him though. Maybe someday I will.

Cole meets George Barris, 1994. *Cole & Susan Foster collection*

THE 1954 CHEVY SHOP TRUCK

The reason that Billy called me in the first place was my '54 Chevy pickup. I had wanted a shop truck for a long time, but when I was ready to buy one, I looked all over town but couldn't turn up anything for sale. I wasn't that particular on what year it was. That model Chevy was made from 1949 to late 1954 when they changed the grille. I did find a few models with the curved corner windows, but I was going to chop it, so I wanted a three-window, period.

The only one I knew of belonged to Butch Hurlhey, best known for his work with Rod Powell. It was just the rattiest-ass truck in the world. It barely ran, and it didn't have a wiper motor: It had some weird, rigged-up mechanism, and he had to pull a stick back and forth to work the wipers. It was a real shit box, painted three different colors, but I really wanted one. I had this nice '57 Buick hardtop, a four-door, but it was just a cream puff. It was never going to be a car that I was going to do anything to, so I flat-ass traded it straight across for the truck. I think Butch felt bad about it, but how could he say no? I reassured him that it was cool and I knew I was on the bad end of the deal, but I really wanted the truck.

For a while, I drove it like it was when we first traded, but it didn't even run on all six cylinders. I yanked the motor for a late-model 250-inch six-cylinder. I bought a manifold and put my nice Holley two-barrel on it with a

header, dual exhaust, and a Turbo 350 transmission. So it was the same ratty truck, but now it ran well. Then I put it down another week and changed out the rearend. I did it a little at a time because it was my transportation. I would be at the shop for four-day stretches, and that's when I'd do the work. Finally it was time to chop the top. Jesse Cruz said, "You should put a top inside of a top and make it like a metal headliner. We could paint it all pearl like an amusement park ride." I also ended up doing the dashboard and frenching the seats in. It was nice, but I didn't really create it to be as well-received as it was. Of everything I've ever done, people really remember that truck. It's funny how sometimes you don't try to impress, but people still dig it.

One of the first people to hit me up for that thing was Jesse James. At that time he was a semi-unknown motorcycle guy who I knew through my friend Rob Fortier. They went to school together. Rob said, "Hey, my friend Jesse wants to trade you a bike for that truck," but I said no. His bikes are cool and everything, but I needed to get around, and I couldn't have a motorcycle as my only form of transportation. He was very determined, though. Finally, years had gone by and I just wasn't showing the truck love any more, but he still had love for it, so I let it go. I think he really digs it, so I'm happy he has it.

continued on page 52

The '54 Chevy shop truck in progress. Cole traded a "cream puff" '57 Buick hardtop for the truck, which he describes as "just the rattiest-ass truck in the world. . . . I knew I was on the bad end of the deal, but I really wanted the truck." *Cole & Susan Foster collection*

The shop truck was chopped three and a half inches. Cole lowered the truck with a Mustang II IFS and by C'ing the frame in the rear. In the rear Cole lowered the stock window to the beltline to match the rest of the glass. The taillights are 1940s-era Harley-Davidson. *Rob Fortier*

Next spread: Headlight rings came from a shoebox Ford, and the pushbutton door openers are Lincoln NOS. Of the unique paint, Cole says, "I went down to the local paint shop and I mixed it myself. I substituted white pearl for the metallic silver, which gave it that real iridescent, surreal look. . . I ended up spraying that thing with pure red toner and a ton of white pearl with some satin clear over it." *Rob Fortier*

continued from page 48

The paint job on it is unique. When I did the purple on my '54 Chevy, it only went to that one event. It's a shame that not too many people ever saw it, because it was just beautiful. So when I painted the truck, which wasn't much later, I went down to the local paint shop and I mixed it myself. I substituted white pearl for the metallic silver, which gave it that real iridescent, surreal look. Then I found clears that would go on flat and not change the color and be nice and even. Erik Solorio ended up spraying that thing with pure red toner and a ton of white pearl with some satin clear over it. I chromed the bumpers and the grille, but I knew it was never going to be a show truck—it was as done as I was going to get it. I took it to the Paso show, and it was a big hit when it was just my work truck.

The roof was really tough because you're working on your back. I had some scaffolding running through the cab, and it was just miserable, eating Bondo and primer. I went down to the local Salvation Army and got a kid's diving mask. It didn't have a snorkel, but it was sealed tight over my nose and my eyes, and I had a mask over my mouth. I remember lying on my back for a couple days, blocking that thing out. Just terrible. But it was worth it. The interior looked Deco.

I searched the swap meets for the right pieces; it didn't matter what brand they were. I've never been very year- or brand-correct. I just trust my eyes. On the truck, I settled on Pontiac gauges and extended the glove box and made my own little garnish chrome piece for it to match. It had Harley-Davidson taillights—just little things like that. I used 1950 Ford headlight rings and moved the bumpers down and fabricated a pan in the back. It was a simple truck, but a hit for sure, I think because it just

didn't have any big mistakes on it. When I see other people's cars and bikes, the first things that stick out are the little mistakes. So when I critique my own stuff, I eliminate what looks wrong to my eye, and it seems like a lot of people agree with me.

I think the reason the shop truck was in so many magazines is because when people came by the shop it was always there. Customers' cars are only at the shop for a short time. You burp them, pat them on the ass, and send them away. But the truck was always there, and it was one of the first cars ever shown in satin paint—that was what really made it a hit. No one was doing that back then. It was even difficult for Rob to convince his bosses, the editors of *Street Rodder* and *Custom Rodder*, to let what was basically a primered vehicle in, no matter how well it was done. But it photographed well, and I think when they saw the pictures, they gave it their blessing.

Back then, it was a struggle trying to do something different. But I'll always remember that Rod Powell would let us put our half-finished cars in his shows, and in the 1980s, you just didn't do that. His shows really were the first "primer nationals," as far as I'm concerned. To tell you the truth, I love looking at cars that are under construction more than I do ones that are finished, because then I get to finish them in my head. I get to paint them whatever color I want to. Sometimes people look at my stuff in progress, and the first thing they ask is, "What color is it going to be?" because it's just not done to them, it's not beautiful if it's not painted, I guess. I love things that are under construction, and I'm always grateful that Rod encouraged us to bring our cars in at any stage, as long as they didn't catch on fire!

Howard's Upholstery did the shop truck's Naugahyde interior. The gauges are '50 Pontiac; the wheel is '50 Buick. Cole extensively modified the stock dashboard. *Rob Fortier*

Next to the paint, perhaps the most commented-upon feature of the Chevy shop truck is the steel headliner. Cole credits Jesse Cruz for the inspiration. "He said we could paint it all pearl like an amusement park ride." The Chevy LUV seatback is frenched into the back of the headliner piece. *Rob Fortier*

CHAPTER FOUR

FREE AT LAST

With the transformation from five-window to three-window on the Hammett '36 nearly complete, Cole and Dad take a break to discuss the progress. Cole and the crew have yet to finish lengthening the doors. Steve Stanford's concept drawing for the car is visible on the wall, to right of Rat Fink. *David Perry*

After I became friends with Mike Ness, he invited us down for some Lonely Kings events. We would stay with the Kennedy brothers. They were basically our age, and they didn't take car clubs too seriously. They grew up with cars, too. We were instant friends.

THE 1932 CHEVY NAILHEAD

One day I was hanging around their shop in Pomona and I told them that I always wanted to build a hot rod, but I didn't have the money to pick up a '32 or a '34. They laughed and said, "We've got a car that you can have for a hundred bucks." It was a '32 Chevrolet coupe, already chopped, but it was in really bad shape. It had a sign in the roof insert and one part of the car had been nailed, but I bought it and brought it home in four pieces. I already had Ford frame rails with a fiberglass '27 body on them, so I started with those. I never felt good about that fiberglass body anyway.

Those old Chevrolet bodies are the worst—just a tin shell over a wood frame. There's no structure—that's why there's hardly any of them out there. The '32 Chevy was actually one of the hardest projects I've ever done.

Usually I have the whole thing built in my mind before I start, but there were no good Chevy hot rods to look at, so I didn't really know where to start. So I just started in the front, mocked up a grille shell, and then put in a Buick Nailhead that I had. The body was difficult, because on those Chevrolets there's a big firewall that sticks way inside the engine compartment and looks terrible. There's too much distance between the motor and the windshield, and I wanted a '32 Ford look. So I cut out the old firewall and welded a new one in.

It seemed like everyone bought headers, and wherever they mounted their motor, the headers ended up pointing down, which looked wrong to me. So I built my own because you couldn't buy them for a Buick motor anyway. Most people had cutouts, but I just ran mine open. The car had a manual three-speed in it, so I had to make linkage. The car was unique because it had a Chrysler rearend and a Buick motor, so there wasn't a lot of space to fit much in it. I had to build the floor and the substructure for the doors. It was a fun build, but it was difficult to get all the pieces in the right proportions. I just had to fill in the blanks.

The '32 Chevy Nailhead started with this. "The Kennedy brothers laughed—I mean they were almost crying when I left their place with thing," Cole recalls. *Cole & Susan Foster collection*

"The '32 Chevy was actually one of the hardest projects I've ever done," Cole says. "Usually I have the whole thing built in my mind before I start, but there were no good Chevy hot rods to look at." Cole sold the car to a Harley-Davidson dealer in Italy. *Bo Bertilsson*

I built that thing on a dare. The Kennedy brothers laughed—I mean they were almost crying when I left their place with thing. But they were pleasantly surprised when they finally saw it. Not many custom guys build a killer hot rod, and hot rod guys usually don't build customs. I never felt bound by any of that—I'll build a motorcycle, I'll build a hot rod, I'll build a custom, I'll build a muscle car, I'll build them all. I'll build a new late-model if I want to, and I think I can pull them all off well.

I didn't want the Chevy to be a shit box. There were kids driving around in some really unsafe-looking hot rods with crappy welds and everything. I didn't want to be that guy. I wanted it to look like some badass guy in a little town built it but didn't finish it, like a little racer, not a show car. So I didn't really do any bodywork on it, I just sprayed it DP90 black, but the frame was really well done, my welds were nice, so I did paint that. The

Nailhead was painted gold and had three two-barrels on it. The inside had wooden door panels and an upholstered seat and carpet. It was nothing I was ever going to show, but I did drive it a lot.

One day a guy named Roberto Rossi, who owns a Harley dealership in Mantova, Italy, wanted to come by my place. When he saw the Chevy, he just fell in love with it. He wanted that hot rod bad. It seemed like he only knew one word. He'd look around our shop and just go, "Bellissimo!" I said that I'd think about selling the car, that it was hard for me to part with it. But he was so crazy about it that I finally agreed and gave him a fair price on it. The next day he sent more than half the money in good faith, so I put the car in a container and sent it to Italy. I think the second half of the money came before he even received it. In 2007, he flew Susan and me over there to go hang out with him for a couple of weeks.

Cole cut out the ungainly stock firewall and welded in a new one flush with the cowl. He also fabricated the headers for the Buick Nailhead. *Bo Bertilsson*

The Model A frame was painted in part to show off Cole's welds, but the body simply received a couple coats of DP90. "There were kids driving around in some really unsafe-looking hot rods with crappy welds and everything," Cole says. "I didn't want to be that guy." *Bo Bertilsson*

Cole bought this 1960 Starliner from Kutty Noteboom. Salinas Boys touches include an expanded-metal front grille and a hand-fabricated center grille bar. Stock headlights were swapped out for a pair from an early-'60s Buick. It was originally lowered about six inches by heating the coils up front and adding six-inch lowering blocks in back. Current owner Aaron Kahan of the Burbank Choppers car club has since had airbags installed in the back and has redone the rear leaf springs. *Bo Bertilsson*

The Starliner's rear was shaved of the gas filler and a custom piece was milled to look stock. It goes across without interruption between the taillights, which were were shaped from Lucite and mounted on top of the original flat plastic lenses. *Bo Bertilsson*

THE 1956 F-100

By the time I sold the '32 Chevy, I had built quite a few nice cars, but I still didn't have a customer base. I remember thinking, "When I am I going to get a break?" One day this guy walked into the shop and introduced himself. He had seen something I did, probably Jerry Wilkinson's Cadillac, and looked me up. He told me he wanted to do an F-100. Now, I don't like those trucks very much, and I'd heard the same story a hundred times—guys would come in and talk a big game, but it usually didn't lead to anything. But I gave him the little shop tour anyway, which usually ended with me showing them my '54 because it had a nice paint job and was finished. I said, "I don't know how far you want to go with your truck. Maybe this is a little extreme, a paint job like this." But he said, "No, I want it *at least* this nice. I can cover whatever you want to do." Sure enough, he already had the truck, a 1956. He said, "I want late-model stuff, a new motor and nice suspension. I really don't have a budget." That was my introduction to Sal Tarantino.

You couldn't tell by looking at him, but he was a big fish in this small town, and it turned out to be a great experience. For two years, Cory and I put our hearts and souls into that truck. He let me do whatever I wanted to with it, and I probably pushed him farther than what he originally wanted, but I knew that this was my shot to make the hot rod world take a good look at me.

I remember that he liked the way the truck sat, but it was ten inches off the ground and there was not a chance that I was leaving it. I play with customers in situations like that. I replaced my shocks with threaded rods, and every time he came in this thing would be just a half inch lower, but it was so gradual that he didn't notice. And so he got used to it being low.

Sal also wanted reverse chromes like the coupe on *American Graffiti*, but I knew those wheels would just kill the truck. Sal also loved the big goofy truck taillights that

continued on page 64

The F-100's fully modified chassis featuring a TCI four-link in back along with TCI independent frontend. Disc brakes at all corners help stop the truck when it's being motivated by a Ford 5.0-liter 302-ci crate mill. Even dad Pat had a hand in the truck, fabricating the custom gas tank. *Cole & Susan Foster collection*

"To this day, I think the F-100 is probably the nicest thing I've ever done," Cole says of the truck that earned the Chip Foose Design Excellence Award. *Rob Fortier*

Previous spread: The award-winning Sal Tarantino F-100. Nosed, filled, corners rounded, bed channeled—the epitome of style. Jesse Cruz sprayed the bronze pearl paint. *Rob Fortier*

Above: The Tarantino F-100's leather interior was sewn by Bill Mangers, who was also responsible for stitching a number of Bill Cushenbery customs through the years. *Rob Fortier*

continued from page 60

say "Ford" on them. I can't stand them, but he had to have them. I suggested we try something else, but he was insistent. So I made some taillights out of '36 lenses and asked him to at least look at them, if he didn't like them we'd change them back. It was silent for a minute, and he said, "Okay, you got me. They're bitchin'."

I was trying to think of a way to get around the reverse chromes. I ended up with some wheels that had '48 caps on them but thought the truck would need wheels that made it look tougher, and not just some champagne-colored steels on a bronzed truck. I painted the wheels black and left beauty rings on them so that they didn't look like NASCAR wheels. That just made the truck for me, and Sal agreed. To this day, I think that truck is probably the nicest thing I've ever done. Whenever I would get away from it for a while, then see it again, I just couldn't believe we built it.

I took it to the Oakland Roadster Show, our first time back after that whole Rick Perry deal, but he was gone by then and new people were running it. I had two kids working for me, 17 and 18 years old. I don't even know if these two had ever been to a car show before. I do know that they had never even waxed a car before in their life. We got there a little bit late, and they got the carpet down where the promoter told me to park. He gave me a hard time, gave me a big sigh like, "What do you want?" I started to wonder, "God, what's up with these promoters? We're like the rock bands at their concert, and they treat us like dirt."

But I wasn't some scared kid this time, so I told him, "Hey, man, knock that off right now. Yeah, yeah, you had a tough day—I've had a tough month. You're having one stressful day, and I've had a month of them." He didn't like that too much, but he showed me where to park. So, I put the truck there, and the guy comes back with this clipboard and says, "I didn't tell you there, I told you over there." So he moved me to some crap spot, and I thought, "Here we go again. Last place." I just put the carpet down, opened one door, and left. I didn't come back until Sunday night. Five days that thing sat there. I came back for the awards ceremony, and I remember sitting there and the truck category came up. It didn't win anything like best interior, best motor, or anything, but I guess the truck with the highest points wins the entire category.

Then, Chip Foose, whom I'd never met, got onstage to explain why he picked certain cars for various awards. When he named Sal's truck for the *Chip Foose Design Excellence Award*, it was a big honor. And the promoter just kissed my ass.

The truck was super-fine. I don't know how to explain it, but I changed every angle of how the body was mounted, made my own bumpers, spent a lot of time on the engine compartment, really thought out the interior. We made a bed from scratch. Bumper brackets too. It had a lot of slick features. I used ball detents with skateboard bearings in the tailgate, so there were no latches. Chip asked if he could really take a good look at it because you can't really touch the vehicles

during the show. He climbed inside, and he was very complimentary. I'll never forget when he got out, he shut the door, and he looked at me funny and asked, "Can I do that again?" I asked, "What?" and he said, "Can I open and shut the door?" He opened it and shut it again and said, "That's the nicest door I've ever felt in my whole life." What a compliment. He's been around the nicest cars in the world. Ever since then, he's been very cool. I've called him for advice about doing design work for companies, and he's always returned my calls and given me great advice.

That truck was a huge turning point, because finally I had a guy—Sal—who believed in me. He didn't even know me that well, but he gave me a shot, and I'll always be grateful to him. Eric Stein had helped me out with the shop as a kid, and now I had a guy who helped me shift into high gear, giving me a shot to build a world-class hot rod, and I think I succeeded.

The F-100 is full of subtle touches, like ball-detent tailgate mechanisms, custom-made taillight lenses, and door latches that prompted Chip Foose to call the doors the nicest he'd ever operated. *Rob Fortier*

Henry Gong's 1956 Nomad was the former Goodies Speed Shop
car in Salinas. What was intended to be a quick repaint and
interior soon snowballed. The handle on the rear gate was
removed and replaced with another rib piece. *Giuseppe Roncen*,
Freeway *and* Kustom *magazines*

Henry Gong's Nomad in progress. *Cole & Susan Foster collection*

To retain a stock appearance in the interior, Cole modified the AC ducts. Howard's Upholstery handled the vinyl interior, all in keeping with the new color combo on the formerly orange wagon. *Giuseppe Roncen*, Freeway *and* Kustom *magazines*

Mooneyes finned aluminum valve covers and a Polynesian-themed air cleaner from Alan Johnson Hot Rods are a few of the modern conceits on the bog-block that had been swapped into the car back in the 1950s. *Giuseppe Roncen*, Freeway *and* Kustom *magazines*

Cole does his best DeNiro. *Zap Teshima*

COLE FOSTER IS THE REAL DEAL. *What you see is what you get. No posing allowed. Dickies pants, Vans slip-ons, starched white tee shirt, a Marlboro red, and Murray's pomade in his hair is how he came out of the womb, I think. Before the "rat rod" scene took off full speed in the 1990s, Cole was building, fabricating, and painting traditional customs and hot rods in his Salinas shop because he liked the way they looked. Apparently, everyone else did too. Cole's '54 Chevy sled, which he started building in the late '80s, is as perfect as perfect gets in my book. It still wins custom awards at shows 20 years later.*

It's rare when you find a cat like Cole who can work metal into sculptures and work you into a lather with his dry wit. I seek him out at shows just to sit down and laugh and forget the stress and strain of everyday life. The '36 Ford he built for Kirk Hammett would make Rodin or Da Vinci jealous.

Street cred? Yeah he's got it in spades. How many guys do you know who toured the country at age eighteen, crewing on one of history's most revered Funny Cars? If you were hanging with Raymond Beadle, "Waterbed" Fred Miller, and the whole Blue Max team at age eighteen, you came, you saw, and you conquered.

If you want to know how your car or bike should look and sit, ask Cole. If you want to know what direction the custom car or custom bike scene is going, ask Cole. Better yet, watch him work. If you want a polished aluminum cowboy hat or bikini, he does those too. He's the one . . . he's the one.

—John Drummond, Goodguys Rod & Custom Association

THE KIRK HAMMETT 1936 FORD

A year or so after Billy and I had talked about doing a car together, ZZ Top was playing in Oakland, so his secretary, Denise, set me up with tickets. After the show, I went backstage to a little meet-and-greet area where you might be lucky to shake a few hands. I told one of the bouncers "Just tell Billy that Cole's here. I know him," and typically the guy said, "Everyone knows him, kid." When Billy came out, he was with the bouncer, and he saw me, ran over, and hugged me. Then he took me back to where there was a festive little scene going on. Then Billy said, "Hey, y'all, listen up," and they all got quiet. "I want you to meet the baddest custom builder on the West Coast—Cole Foster."

I looked around and noticed the guys from Journey, people you might expect to see there, but there were also two guys with black fingernails. I'd seen one of them before but couldn't place him. Then I figured out it was Kirk Hammett from Metallica. I could tell that he maybe wanted to talk. Finally he told me he was going to get his wife, Lani, a GTO convertible. "Can you paint it black for me, like my nails?"

I got to B.S.'ing with him, and I gave him my card. This sort of thing happens a million times, and you never expect to hear from them again. But the next day, I got a nice voicemail: "Hi, this is Kirk Hammett. It was a pleasure to meet you, and I'm real serious about this thing. Give me a call."

Kirk and Lani came to the shop with the GTO. They bought it from a roadie or someone, and it wasn't in the best shape. Kind of a polished turd. It was bright,

Converting the five-window to a three-window necessitated moving the back half of the roof section forward three and a half inches. This removed what Cole refers to as the car's "bed head." *Bo Bertilsson*

fire-engine red, but the body was pretty wavy. A lot of people overlook that in what otherwise seems like a decent car. I told him a good paint job is just like a pond in the morning—not a ripple in it. It reflects perfectly. If you throw a pebble in it, it gets ripples and the reflection distorts. That's what their car was—very distorted. So, I did the car, and I kind of overdid it. I guess I don't know how to do it any other way—it's a little more work, but better things usually come of it.

Lani is probably more of a motorhead than Kirk, but he dug what we were doing, and started grumbling a little bit about doing a custom. So, I signed him up for a subscription to *The Rodder's Journal* and let him do his homework. When we would check in, he would talk more and more about doing a car, and I steered him toward a '36 Ford because they're one of my favorites, and I really wanted to do one.

I always made it okay for him to be new to it all, like I would be about music. I always said, "Just tell me whatever you want, and I'll never laugh at your for anything you say. I don't care if you don't know every year, and I will never put you down like I'm a know-it-all. If you have an idea, let me know."

But sometimes Kirk would get a little off track and come up with something like, "What about a spider web this or that?" I'd say, "Look at your house, Kirk. You don't have any spider web stuff. You have all this classy art deco furniture. Let's stick to that." Or he'd read an issue of *Lowrider* and ask, "What do you think of those wire wheels with the gold trim around them?" I'd say, "They're cool on a '64 Impala, but really, Kirk, try to get into the mindset of. . . ." Then I'd think about what would point him back in the right direction. "What I'm thinking is a blacked-out spooky car, and no one knows who this guy is driving it. It's a retro-future ride that's sinister and classy." Just like the furniture in his house. Once I got him on that page, he stopped thinking outside of his tastes.

I knew it was going to be a long build. First, it was hard to find a three-window coupe. I had one lined up. An older guy said he'd sell it. I even got the money from Kirk to go buy it, but then when I got there, he changed his mind. Now I have a wad of money in my pocket but no car. Eventually I found another three-window. I bought it and stripped it, but it was just junk. Now, I'm really in trouble. I've spent Kirk's money, so I had to go buy a car for him on my own.

Aaron Elliott, one of the Salinas Boys on staff for the Hammett build. *Cole & Susan Foster collection*

With the windshield surround for Hammett's '36. A new laser-cut surround was worked over by hand. *Cole & Susan Foster collection*

Cole and his dad hand-formed the floor. *David Perry*

So I drove all the way to Riverside to look at a three-window. I brought the trailer with, and when I got there, it was a nice car, but it was a five-window. But it was such a nice car, and I had a three-window at the shop that wasn't worth a dime, I figured I had enough to make it a three-window. I dragged it home, and I don't even think that Kirk knew that I messed up the deal. I spent my own money, but I had to fix my mistake.

The car took a few years to build, but we're a small shop. It's usually me and another guy or two. And you're always waiting for something, so you always have another project going at the same time, and you're going back and forth. It's very labor-intensive. With the '36, I wanted to make connections with people in the industry, so I put out a résumé of what I was doing. I already knew in my head what the car was going to look like, but people wanted to see it on paper, so I had Keith Weesner draw it up on my instruction. We communicated well, and he knows his stuff.

Mainly, I wanted people to be interested in Kirk's car as something that they would want to be associated with. And, frankly, I wanted to meet people for future projects.

Note from Pat to Cole. The Hammett '36. *David Perry*

I called Roy Brizio, a nice guy who absolutely didn't know me, but he took the time to explain how these things work. It's nice when you call someone, and they call you right back and it's no B.S.—they give you straight answers. And you love a guy who's secure enough to give out information. I'm no threat to Roy Brizio. He's good at what he does, he's solid, and he shared information with me. I would do the same for someone else. It was a great experience, and I really didn't compromise the build if somebody gave me parts. Plus, I only went after things that I really wanted.

I wanted a basic chassis, so I called up TCI, but I knew they're not set up for customs. You can't get their chassis low enough—it's a coil-over, four-bar car where the suspension hangs way underneath. It's good for a hot rod but not for a custom. They thought I was nuts, but I told them I wanted a chassis that was just tacked together so that I could break the tacks. Then I had Dad come out and not totally change it around, but kick up the frame rails, move the motor up, and make it clean underneath so that nothing hung down.

I also got a number of other companies involved in the project. Ford, Don Armstrong with US Radiator, Wheels of Steele, and Coker Tires all helped out. PPG opened the doors to their paint department, and Kicker car audio totally wanted in on the project. It's cool when people are excited to the point that they even offer to fly out to help. It's also nice to have a relationship in which people are accommodating, because I'm picky. I want to sort through three different tires before I pick one.

I had a kid, Aaron Elliott, working for me at the time, and Dad just took to the kid. I was traveling to promote the Blue Bike, and my dad really adopted Aaron. They did a lot of the chassis work and mounted the body.

People think it was a huge deal to chop a five-window. It wasn't easy, but I had Aaron build some fixtures to move the roof forward and get it to fit. My friend Chris Prokapow has a really nice '36 three-window. I really like its window openings, so I asked for a template. When Aaron and I got through the chopping, we had to take sedan doors and make them three-window doors. But that was a purely mechanical exercise.

Discussing the arrival
of a new part with
dad Pat as a pair of
attention-grabbing
cars take shape: the
Hammett '36 in the
foreground and the
Henry Gong '56 Nomad
in the background.
David Perry

We did a normal chop on it, three and a half inches or so, then we put it out in the alley, took some pictures, and went back and studied them. I wasn't very happy with the back of the roof. It had a little too much bubble to it, so I re-chopped the back just to take the bed head off the thing. I study this sort of thing a lot when I'm working on a car. I try to look at the whole picture and how everything fits together, and I thought the beltline was too big right under the window. I also wanted the roof a little bit lower, but I didn't want the windows any lower. I always see cars that are chopped a little bit too much, and they look too fat above the door. My first thought was to thin out the door surround. I just took three-quarters of an inch out of the beltline, which chopped the roof another three-quarters of an inch but left the side windows the same. It gave the top the illusion of being a lot lower than it is. If I didn't tell anyone I did this, I really don't think they'd notice.

After changing the beltline, I was really adamant about changing the front windshield. The stock windshield frame is big and it makes the car look like an armored car when you're done with the chop. So we made our own stainless-steel surround. It was lasered from a single piece of stainless steel—I just filed it to give it a little bit of a crown. We also moved the back window down a couple of inches. So basically, we took out the window openings, chopped the car, then put the openings back in, not allowing the amount of the chop dictate their size.

Art Chrisman is my total hero. I was about halfway done with Sal's F-100 and there was talk about it possibly being in *The Rodder's Journal* when the magazine showed up and Art's yellow F-100 was on the cover. That truck set the bar. Dad was really good friends with Art and he told me that he saw him at the races and said, "Hey, Art, my kid's building an F-100. He said he's going to blow your ass off with it." Art said, "Good luck," and they laughed about it.

I brought Sal's F-100 to the Hot Rod Reunion in Bakersfield, and Art looked at it. If he really likes something, he leaves a note on it that says "Art approved." I still have the note he left on that truck.

Sal's F-100 never made it into *The Rodder's Journal*, but by the time I was doing Kirk's '36, the editor, Geoff Miles, and the publisher, Steve Coonan, at least knew who I was. I told them about the '36. I also decided to keep it in bare metal because I like the way those cars look. What a pain that turned out to be. That car probably took me a third of the time longer because of it. There were times we could have been doing bodywork but we had to leave it in that stage. Even keeping the body clean in the shop is a hassle. I wouldn't recommend it to anyone. There's no reason to keep a car in bare metal. I think most people would do it if they knew it would get them in *The Rodder's Journal*, but I don't think I'd do it again.

I'm thankful that Kirk gave me the opportunity to do that car. When your reputation's not built yet, you can still cause a little hype, but you better be able to back it up, and I think we totally backed it up with that car. Kirk gave me 100-percent freedom. Hopefully people will continue to let me do my thing. When they do, I don't think I disappoint.

Blues legend and custom car aficionado Jimmie Vaughan drops by the shop in January 2005 with Hammett's '36 still in progress. *Cole & Susan Foster collection*

Opposite: Making order and cleanliness a habit. Cole performs one of the customizer's more mundane tasks at the old shop. *David Perry*

The car much as
it appeared in *The
Rodder's Journal*
No. 27, sans wheel
covers. This high
front-three-quarter
view accentuates
the tapered running
boards and the
wedge-lie channel:
zero inches up front,
three in the rear.
Zap Teshima

The 1930s-era Chevy
commercial headlight
buckets with rings of
the same make and
vintage rest in coves
that Cole fabricated.
Zap Teshima

Readying the world's most famous bare-metal car for its black paint. Of keeping the car in bare metal, Cole simply says it was a "pain in the ass." *The Flyin' Dutchman, a.k.a. Maurice Van den Tillaard*

Previous spread and above: Jesse Cruz sprayed the black paint at Don Orosco's facilities. *Max Trono*, Kustom *magazine*

Left: Studebaker taillights and Cole's handmade bezels are set in the reshaped rear fenders. *Max Trono*, Kustom *magazine*

Opposite: The custom grille from Grille Art Company of Idaho, along with the stock horn grilles, which Cole left intact, help testify to Cole's vision that the car reflect its owner's affinity for art deco. *Bo Bertilsson*

Cole found inspiration from various sources for the interior. The dash panels are '56 Olds modified to carry the art deco theme indoors. The steering wheel is of English descent and modified by Cole, who also shaped the marbled knob atop the Gennie shifter.
Jesus Espinoza, DeadendMagazine.com

The reshaped rear fenders with their custom-fabricated skirts belie Cole's appreciation for European coachbuilders as much as any direct lineage to his American custom car forebears. *Bo Bertilsson*

The spun-aluminum wheel covers were a swap-meet find. Cole welded in the beauty rings, and the acrylic center emblems are shoebox Ford horn buttons. The tires are Coker. Those louvers also show Cole isn't afraid to go across the pond for inspiration. They're fabricated from stock '36 louvers. *Max Trono*, Kustom *magazine*

Above: Hammett's only requirement for the car was this custom guitar case, which allows him to plug and play anywhere he pleases. The car is outfitted with Kicker audio components with custom cases by former Salinas Boy Thomas Torjeson. *Max Trono, Kustom magazine*

Left: Making a last-minute adjustment to the Hammett '36 as Thomas Torjeson looks on during a photo shoot for the book *Hot Rod Kings. Kevin Thomson*

Cole's intent: "kind of a retro-future ride that's sinister and classy." *Jesus Espinoza, DeadendMagazine.com*

Sometimes Cole builds 'em for himself. Dave DeLuxe captured him with his '52 Panhead in April 2004. *Dave "DeLuxe" Wiltgen*

CHAPTER FIVE

THE BIKES

he F-100 was the big turning point. It bolstered my confidence and gave me some street rod cred. After that, I got a shot from a major company to build a motorcycle. I think I hit a home run on that, too.

THE BLUE BIKE

The story behind the Blue Bike is interesting. I was doing my car thing at the shop, and this guy named Eric Feltner was hanging out. He had a friend who needed some paint work and who introduced me to a guy who worked for Custom Chrome, the world's biggest seller of aftermarket V-twin parts. This guy was a little bit star struck by the current bike builders like Jesse James. He really put them on a pedestal. I would tell him I could build one of those bikes, and he would laugh at me and tell me I was a "car guy."

But I kept asking him more questions about what he did and why certain guys got to build bikes for Custom Chrome. He told me that Custom Chrome would give known bike builders all the parts they wanted. The guy would build a bike, making some stuff but also using parts out of the Custom Chrome catalog and using their motors and transmissions and whatever. When the bike was done, Custom Chrome toured it for the season with the builder's name on it and then gave the bike back to the builder.

So I decided I wanted to do a bike, but this guy insisted Custom Chrome would never agree to let me do one, that I was a car guy. I asked him to get me a meeting with them. I persisted and gave him some magazines with my cars in them so that they would know I wasn't just some nobody. I also told him I could get them in the car magazines. Finally, he went to their marketing department with the little portfolio that I put together, and they agreed to a meeting.

Well, now I was in trouble because I knew I couldn't get their bike in car magazines. I called my friend Rob Fortier at *Street Rodder* and asked him if he could put a bike in the magazine. He told me that there was no chance his editor would go for it and they even had a "no bike" rule. Here I am with this meeting coming up with Custom Chrome based on the promise that I'm going to put their bikes all over car magazines, which I can't. So I wrote an e-mail saying, "I'm Rob Fortier from

McMullen-Argus Publishing. I've featured everything Cole has done in the last ten years and I would love to see him do a bike project." But it didn't *say Street Rodder* would feature the bike, it only led them to *believe* that they would feature it. I asked Rob to send the e-mail and he was really reluctant, but finally he did.

Joel, the guy who set up the meeting, kept talking about Jesse James and tattoos, and I got to thinking, "I don't have any tattoos, and I'm not missing teeth or anything—maybe I should bring somebody with me—a sidekick to be the gnarly guy." I called up pro skateboarder Jason Jessee and asked if he'd come to the meeting and just hang out. "You don't have to say a word—just be the guy that looks like a biker."

Jason agreed, and I brought my portfolio again. They asked me what I wanted to build, and I said, "Well, I've got five bikes in my head I can build right away." I told them I had taken a good look at the bike magazines and that I wouldn't do anything like what Jesse and the other guys were doing. I said, "If choppers are mean dangerous, loud, fast, I'm going to give you all that, but I'm going to go in a different direction. It'll be loud and look dangerous, but I'm going to do it my way." The car magazines were their big selling point, so I totally B.S.'d them, really.

I also asked them about designing parts and whether the guys that built bikes for them ever made parts for them too. They said, "Yeah, yeah, yeah," so I think they were half-B.S.'ing me, too. I got to thinking that every part I built for the bike was going to get in their catalog and I'd get royalties. This is it.

I still remember the only thing Jason said at the whole meeting. He started to talk, and they interrupted him, and then said, "No, go ahead." These six business guys are looking at him and he chokes for a second and then says, "Well, you guys could finally be leaders instead of followers. Instead of just copying what's popular, Cole's going to make something popular, and you guys will be the first with it." They tilted their heads like, "Yeah, okay," and we left the meeting with a deal.

So I had free rein with Custom Chrome's motorcycle catalog, but I didn't know what I was looking at. Mechanically, I didn't have any problem building a bike, but if you really look at the catalogs, they're all based on Harley-Davidson production years. It would have been a lot easier to start with a 2001 Harley-Davidson then go to the catalog. When you start with nothing and try to mix and match all these different parts that are listed by years, it can be confusing. Something would look cool in the catalog, but then I'd get it, and it would look like it belonged on a diesel truck.

That bike probably became Custom Chrome's biggest hit ever, and it definitely opened doors for me to continue doing it. When the bike went to the Powersports Expo in Indianapolis, Custom Chrome flipped. They had been like some ugly duckling, and all of a sudden they were this beauty queen. They just didn't know what to do with themselves having all these people looking at it, asking who built it. I was scheduled to go just to Indianapolis with them, but Daytona Bike Week was soon after that,

and when they saw how popular the bike was at Indy, they asked me go to Daytona Beach.

The bike got a lot of press because Custom Chrome brought in this kid from nowhere and he hit it out of the park. People at Custom Chrome were asking, "When did this happen, and why didn't we know about it?"

But it was a great experience, and Custom Chrome ended up making a gas tank based on the one I did for the Blue Bike. It's been a great relationship. That was a big step in my career, being able to go into a field that I was absolutely not in and be sort of a trendsetter with that bike. If you open a copy of *Easyriders* from before that bike came out and you open one now, you'll see a lot of bikes that were influenced by that Blue Bike.

The Blue Bike epitomizes a combination of classic styling and twenty-first-century innovation. Weighing in at less than 300 pounds and outfitted with an 88-ci RevTech, the bike's power-to-weight ration ain't too shabby, either. *Giuseppe Roncen,* Freeway *and* Kustom *magazines*

Designing that bike, I looked toward a few different things, like I do with anything I build—racing, for sure, and history, what guys were doing at home back in the day. A V-twin is a throwback in itself—really super low-tech—so I wasn't going to try to make it something it isn't. I wasn't going to make a super-slick, modern-looking motorcycle and then basically put an air-compressor motor in it.

Don't get me wrong—I love the sound of a V-twin, and I love the fact that they haven't changed. But I try to break something down to its essence and remain true to that—what is it, what could it be, what could it have been? This whole industry is built off of Harley-Davidson—it's still cool and it's still recognizable as a Harley-Davidson after all these years. That can't be said for a lot of things. If you lift the hood on a modern Chevrolet, even though it basically has a small-block Chevy in it, there's so much crap bolted to it, you can't even see the motor. Imagine lifting the hood on a new GM and it looks just like a 327—that's what a Harley still does. To make all that old and new work together is one of the hardest things to do. It's easy to do a 1952 Harley Davidson. It's also easy to drift off and get sidetracked.

The half-width exposed primary, chain drive, and four-speed gearbox were an exercise by Cole and the boys to keep the Blue Bike narrow. Jason Jessee was instrumental in helping Cole get the go-ahead from Custom Chrome to do the bike. *Giuseppe Roncen*, Freeway *and* Kustom *magazines*

As with all Salinas Boys vehicles, the Blue Bike features a fair amount of Salinas Boys tinwork, including the rear fender with its subtle integral taillight. It's a design touch Cole would carry over to the Special K project. *Giuseppe Roncen*, Freeway *and* Kustom *magazines*

Opposite: Less is more. The Blue Bike's Salinas Boys pipes are short and sweet, the Salinas Boys–cast beehive oil bag a timeless design, and all other details exquisite. *The Flyin' Dutchman, a.k.a. Maurice Van den Tillaard*

The rear axle features a jointed retainer/adjuster, and the forty-spoke wheel wears an M&H Racemaster slick. *The Flyin' Dutchman, a.k.a. Maurice Van den Tillaard*

A good look at the Blue Bike's integrated "floating" hand levers and the Salinas Boys marbleized acrylic grips. *The Flyin' Dutchman, a.k.a. Maurice Van den Tillaard*

Previous spread: Zero rake, zero stretch—even from this dramatic angle. Up front, a twenty-inch Avon complements the eighteen-inch M&H slick out back. This view provides a backside look at the disc brake styled to give the appearance of a drum from the left side of the bike. *Giuseppe Roncen,* Freeway *and* Kustom *magazines*

With fellow Sinner club member Chopper Dave at the Mooneyes Yokohama Hot Rod & Custom Show, December 2004. *Cole & Susan Foster collection*

Opposite top: Big in Japan. Cole's fans come out to see him at the Mooneyes Yokohama Hot Rod & Custom Show, December 2004. *Cole & Susan Foster collection*

Opposite bottom: Cole meets one of his favorite bike builders, Zero Engineering's Shinya Kimura. Mooneyes Yokohama Hot Rod & Custom Show, December 2004. *Cole & Susan Foster collection*

ADVENTURES IN LALA LAND

Not long after Motorcycle Mania hit the mainstream when Jesse James did his show—my dad was out working with me. It was right after 9/11. He was building Top Fuel cars, but the phone wasn't ringing because I think everybody was a little bit on pause. I had Kirk's car and the Blue Bike going, so I told my dad, with whom I'd never worked side by side, to come out for a month.

We were cooking away on the Blue Bike when I got a call from Original Productions saying that Jesse James had a new TV show called *Monster Garage*. I told Dad they wanted me to do this TV show, and he asked, "Are they paying you?" I said, "Well, I don't think so." It was just a pilot at that point. Dad asked, "Then why would you go do it?"

Still, I wanted to do it because it was something different. I questioned the producers: "Do you want me to design something?" They said, "No, we just want you to be on the team. Jesse gave us your name." But I just had a hard time conceiving why anyone would want to take, say, a Ford Mustang and mow a golf course with it. Plus, I was busy, so I passed. Later, when I saw it, I immediately got it: It's the whole romanticism of the build process, not the end result.

I was called again for a few different episodes after the show was picked up. I was still busy, but I ended up doing one episode on the first season. We had to put a paddle wheel in the rear of an RX7 and run it in the sand. It wasn't too difficult to fabricate, but there were a lot of different things right from the get-go that weren't very easy to make work well.

I worked with some guys on the show who I thought were really good. Anthony, who works at West Coast Choppers with Jesse, is a great kid, a young guy with a lot of talent and nice demeanor. I wanted to steal him for Salinas Boys. I even told Jesse that: "Hey, man, I'm trying to steal Anthony from you," and he said, "No, leave him alone. He's a good kid." He still works for Jesse in Long Beach.

On the show I also worked with a kid who had racecar fabrication experience and was very, very good. Not that I'm a know-it-all. I learn largely by trial and error—a hillbilly fabricator. I've never taken an engineering course, but I'm good with rudimentary formulas and problem solving because that's what I do every day, so I was given the role of checking everyone out, because this kid was probably a better fabricator than me, but he wasn't very good at problem solving and doing things as simply as possible. Together, I think we came up with some good solutions.

One of my heroes, Lil' John Buttera, was our overseer. He would come in and blow some steam on us. On the final day he told me that I'm just like my dad: I make pretty stuff, but it doesn't work. So I asked, "How much of your stuff worked?" We gave it to each other back and forth, but all in good fun.

Jesse was very cool to me on the show. Once, I went to use his TIG welder, but I hadn't seen the show enough to know that no one touched Jesse's welder. So when I sat down to make something, they all freaked on me. "What do you mean I can't use it? It's a tool. It's here." There wasn't another welder like it on the set, and it happened to be the kind I use every day, so I played along. "Well, screw him. I'm going to use it, and he can tell me if he doesn't want me to." They thought they had a real drama—"He's using the welder. He's going to get his ass reamed by Jesse." I knew better, so I sat down and made whatever I was making, and when Jesse came in, he was stoked. They were bummed there weren't any dramatics.

TV editing can make or break you. On the last night of the show, Buttera tried calling me out for doing something wrong with the chain drive, and I remember absolutely knowing I didn't do it wrong. I heard him ragging about me and thought, "Oh, this is the part where I end up a heel at the end of the show." So, I asked them to explain to me what was going on. Once I got it out of them, I was really deliberate and clear: "So you guys are saying the wheel can't be moved back, that I screwed it up? Can you give me three minutes?" They all had their saws and torches ready to whack off everything I'd worked on for three days.

I dove under that thing with my tools and saw that *they* had it the wrong way, not me, just as I thought.

Next spread: Cole's been a favorite subject of many photographers, and David Perry was one of the first to extensively document Cole and various Salinas Boys creations. Perry captured a reflective Cole with the Blue Bike in the old Salinas Boys space. *David Perry*

They had put the chain on with too much slack. But I adjusted it like they wanted it done and said, "Okay, now slide the wheel back and try to put the chain on." I knew they wouldn't be able to get the chain on because the wheel was now too far back. I said, "Okay, try and put the chain on now," but it wouldn't go on. They were all wondering why, and I told them, "Because now it's too far back. That means I was right. Thank you." Then I carried on with whatever I had been doing. I was confident after that, but there was a moment where I flat-out panicked.

We got the thing going, this heavy convertible trying to run on one tire. It was just goofy. But it was around midnight, and the drama was all real. We had to do some last-minute adjustments, but we loaded the stupid thing on the trailer. Jesse decided we were going to run this thing on the beach at midnight, right on the sand in front of all of these beautiful condos. Of course this RX7 has a Wankel rotary motor, the loudest thing ever on nitrous oxide, but we unloaded it and lit that thing up. The paddle tire that we hooked up to the rear where the trunk is, was like a boat motor that you can lower and raise. We put it all the way down, Jesse hit the throttle, and that thing just dug a hole.

continued on page 106

Just a kid from the Valley with a motorcycle. *The Flyin' Dutchman, a.k.a. Maurice Van den Tillaard*

continued from page 103

So I told Jesse to raise it up and get the thing going then lower the swing arm as he picked up speed to get more of a bite. So, he laced this thing, and it went fifty miles an hour past people making out on the beach. I saw the police lights coming right as we finished. But it made a nice pass. It slung the chains off, but basically it passed its little test.

The funny thing about television, at least for me, is that at first you're so self-conscious that you can't count your fingers or toes, but by the end of the show, you can ham it up or you think you should be directing the show. I did a little thing on a show called *Popular Hot Rodding* with my friends Cameron Evans and Dean Skuza. They featured the truck that we did for Sal Tarantino that won the Oakland Roster Show and the Foose award. It was almost like a television magazine shoot. They went around the car, very detailed, covering each feature. The same production company that did *Popular Hot Rodding* did a show called *Corbin's Ride On*, and I got a call to do that with the Blue Bike.

Above: Cole lets loose on his Trumpet. *Below:* The 1970 Triumph Cole restored for his dad. *Cole & Susan Foster collection*

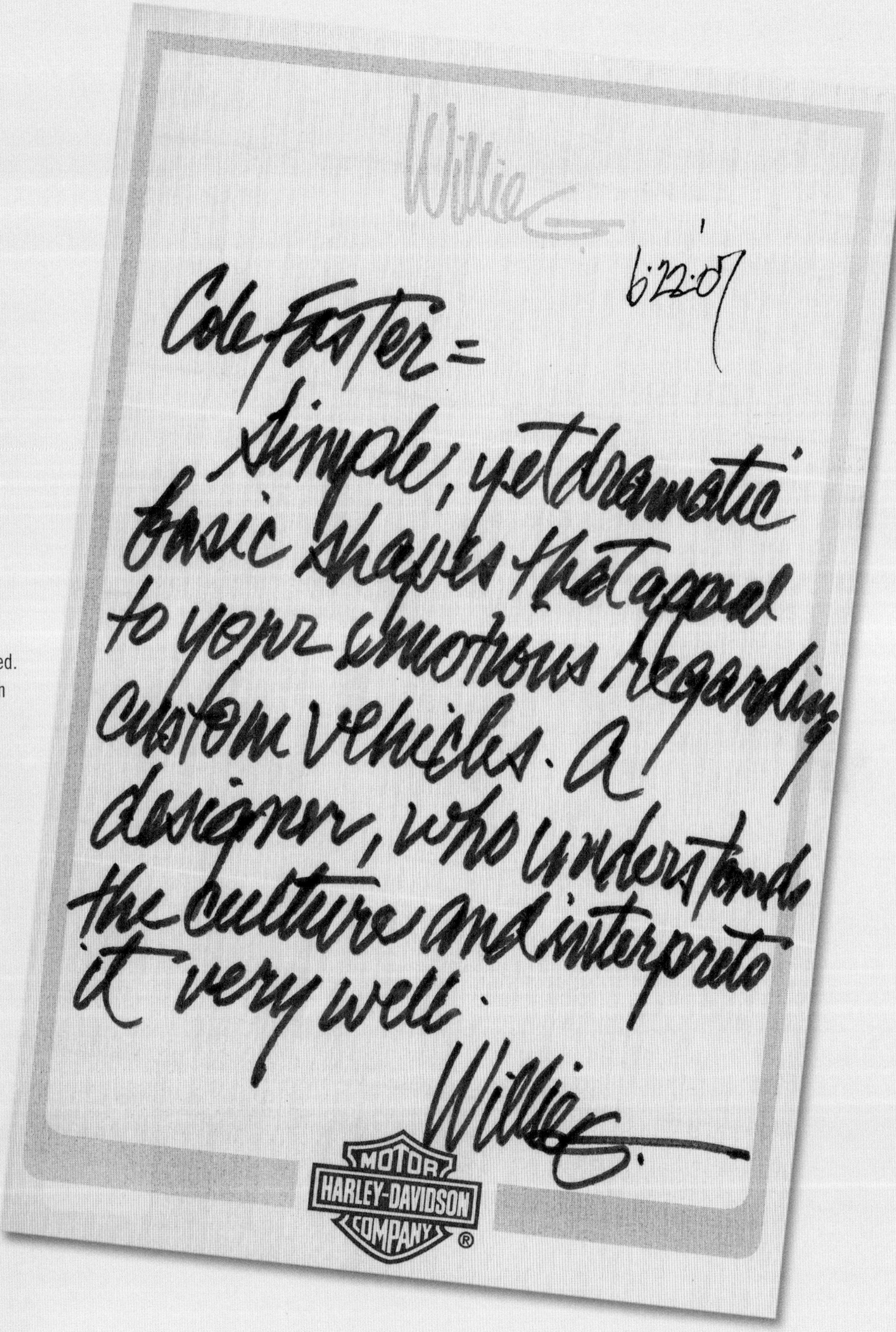

Willie G.

6-22-07

Cole Foster =
    Simple, yet dramatic
basic shapes that appeal
to your emotions regarding
custom vehicles. A
designer, who understands
the culture and interprets
it very well.

Willie G.

MOTOR
HARLEY-DAVIDSON
COMPANY

High praise, indeed.
A testimonial from
one of Cole's
admirers. *Cole
& Susan Foster
collection*

BEAUTIFUL LOSER AND *BIKER BUILD-OFF*

I was flattered to be on *Corbin's Ride On*. The Blue Bike was a hit, but I had gone back to normal work at the shop and eventually some prototype work for Custom Chrome. Soon, a year went by and I hadn't really come out with anything new. Then, all of a sudden, there's *Biker Build-Off* and all these guys I know are getting their own TV shows.

I'd been working hard, but it was all prototype work, which wasn't getting in magazines, so I was bummed, like they forgot about me. Then I got a call from a production company for *Biker Build-Off*, and they said they asked a builder who was on the first season, Hank Young, who his favorite builder was, and he said my name. I'm sure the production company didn't know who I was, but they called me and said Hank was a fan of mine and that they'd love to have me on the show. I was super flattered. I was aware of Hank's work but had never met him, and I thought it would be great.

The big rivalry that's supposed to be between the two guys on the show, is completely fabricated. At least in the case of Hank and me. We were really fans of each other. But I never really saw the show too much and was busy at the time. I kept asking the production company questions. "Guys are really building bikes from scratch in ten days and they have to be painted and rideable?" I signed up and called Steve Belcher at CCI and they sent me some parts, and I hustled up some other parts. Big Mike from BMC Choppers came up with a motor and Mike Corbin was a big help with seats or whatever I needed. I'm a one-off builder, and I certainly didn't have a warehouse full of parts. And once filming starts, you don't have time to order anything because it won't get there in time.

I also didn't have much help at the time. Usually, I have one guy or maybe one guy and a cleanup kid, but that's it. At the time of the *Biker Build-Off* shoot, I had someone coming from Norway to work for me—Thomas Torjeson. He flew in on Saturday, and we started the bike on Monday—he walked right into a TV show his first day

As seen on Discovery Channel! Beautiful Loser was built in ten days per the rules of the hit cable television series *Biker Build-off.* The Flyin' Dutchman, a.k.a. Maurice Van den Tillaard

Beautiful Loser's belt drive was built at Salinas Boys. The oil tank is cast aluminum, also a Salinas Boys item. The seat is Corbin. *The Flyin' Dutchman, a.k.a. Maurice Van den Tillaard*

on the job. It was wild, because I had never worked with the guy. I also brought in some friends of mine for the week. Looking back at other episodes, I would guess 90 percent of the builders probably had their bikes prebuilt before the show and did what they do on a cooking show—laugh, throw all the ingredients together, put it in the oven, and pull out after the next commercial, a beautiful casserole with pineapple slices.

At least I think that's what most people did, but we really had to build this thing in ten days. It was crazy but also fun. I had Job and Thomas working for me, and I brought in David McGuire, a friend from Santa Cruz. Jesse Cruz came in and painted the bike. I dropped off the tin with him at noon the day before it was supposed to run and got it back at noon the next day, then had to assemble it and have it running by midnight. The production staff loved it because everyone else always had their bikes painted on the fifth day and still had five days to put it together. I didn't know any better. They didn't think we'd pull it off, but we did.

Beautiful Loser is based on a Cole-modified Santee soft-tail frame. Wheels are BMC sixty-spokes, front and rear. The Morris mag out back was supplied by J&P Cycles. *The Flyin' Dutchman, a.k.a. Maurice Van den Tillaard*

The bike doesn't look very complicated, but I think we did as much as almost anyone on the show. I just tried to build a nice motorcycle with my style in it. I didn't try to reinvent the wheel or do some way wacky design, like a bike you'd see on a cartoon.

Of course, Hank won. His bike was very nice and a little more clever than mine. We really did ride them 600 miles, all the way from Monterey to San Diego. I don't think Hank or I were ready for that.

After *Biker Build-Off*, I got a call to do a TV commercial for Miller Genuine Draft. By that time, my future wife Susan and I were tight, so I had a good agent, too. By the time she got done negotiating, she got me ten times the amount they offered me at the beginning. It was the largest Miller campaign in Europe—I was on billboards, double-decker busses, and two television commercials.

Anyone who says acting is hard is full of it. I've never been pampered like that my whole life. I had my own assistant who would ask me if I was hungry and a girl for hair and makeup.

Opposite: Power comes via a 96-ci S&S motor mated to a RevTech tranny. *The Flyin' Dutchman, a.k.a. Maurice Van den Tillaard*

Right: Custom Chrome supplied the tank, which Cole and the boys modified. Jesse Cruz provided paint on the project. *The Flyin' Dutchman, a.k.a. Maurice Van den Tillaard*

Beautiful Loser's headlight is also a Custom Chrome product with modifications by Salinas Boys, included the fabricated nacelle.
The Flyin' Dutchman, a.k.a. Maurice Van den Tillaard

This view of Beautiful Loser shows off a number of Salinas Boys touches, including the marbleized grips, the rear fender, and the license-plate surround/taillight. *The Flyin' Dutchman, a.k.a. Maurice Van den Tillaard*

Susan and Cole at the Ultimate Chop awards ceremony, Las Vegas Hard Rock Cafe, April 2005. *Cole & Susan Foster collection*

With Hank Young, en route from Monterey to San Diego, on the *Biker Build-Off* ride, 2004. *Cole & Susan Foster collection*

With Billy Lane at the Ultimate Chop awards ceremony, Las Vegas Hard Rock Cafe, April 2005. *Cole & Susan Foster collection*

Wild Bill Carter lent his talents to Special K's paint. The lace pattern on the Cole Foster Custom Chrome tank required a field trip of Carter. *The Flyin' Dutchman, a.k.a. Maurice Van den Tillaard*

SPECIAL K

My friend Jeff Decker, an amazing sculptor who lives in Utah, had tried several times to build a bike for his wife, Kelly, but they somehow always ended up being his. When he came to me to build a bike for Kelly, I was determined that it really would be hers. This time, Jeff knew he was history by the end of the build because I really kept involving Kelly.

I got Wild Bill Carter to paint it, and he killed it. Bill's a rough guy but a total sweetheart. I told him, "That lace is the most amazing lace I've ever seen," And he said, "You know what the secret is? You got to get it right off the chick, off the dance floor. Man, I went down to Hoochies"—or whatever—"down the street and

I peeled those lace stockings right off the stripper. They got to have that human, you know, oil on them or something."

I was stoked to do a bike with my heroes, Jeff and Bill, and I love Kelly. It's a beauty, with those Performance Machine wheels that Jeff got; they're like twelve-spoke Americans.

As soon as I finished it, it had to go to Michael Lichter's show in Sturgis. Kelly hadn't seen the finished bike, and it was a surprise that it was done. Man, she bawled like a baby. Jeff and I were heroes. It really is her bike—she rides it—and it was a fun one. It ended up being a centerfold in *Easyriders*.

Previous spread: The Special K build took Cole and the boys five months. Cole performed some mods to the rear section of the 2005 Santee rigid frame, shortened the Model K Harley-Davidson frontend, and custom fabricated the headlight nacelle. Jeff Decker fabricated the headlight and cast the outer shell for the oil tank. The seat came from George Atkins in San Jose. The bike was built for Kelly Decker, wife of Utah-based sculptor Jeff Decker. *The Flyin' Dutchman, a.k.a. Maurice Van den Tillaard*

Cole says Jeff Decker picked out the Performance Machine wheels, which recall American Racing twelve-spokes and Cole's obvious drag-racing influences. Both wheels are shod with Avon rubber. *The Flyin' Dutchman, a.k.a. Maurice Van den Tillaard*

Above: Special K includes many features custom fabricated by Cole and Salinas Boys, including the bars, risers, grips, pipes, and pegs. The rear fender with its integrated taillight, however, might be the most sublime. The fender is formed from the spare-tire cover off a '36 Ford; one of Cole's favorite screwdrivers donated the red plastic for the lens. *The Flyin' Dutchman, a.k.a. Maurice Van den Tillaard*

Opposite: Special K's power comes courtesy of a 2005 Harley-Davidson carbureted by an S&S Super E and mounted on a Santee frame. The air cleaner started life as an army canteen. Cole added aluminum, shaped it, bead-blasted it, and polished the scallop element. *The Flyin' Dutchman, a.k.a. Maurice Van den Tillaard*

1941 FLATHEAD

More recently, I built this 1941 Flathead that one of my custom car heroes, Kent Kozera, brought me as a basket case. At first, we were going to just throw it together, but I got a call from *The Horse* magazine just as the parts were coming in, and they asked me if I wanted to be part of the first Smoke Out West build-off with four other builders, including Indian Larry Legacy, for the magazine. This time we'd have eight months to do it, not ten days. At the time, my '52 Panhead was also a basket case, but I wasn't ready to spend the dough or time to get it going, so I remembered Kent's bike. I told Kent about it and offered to step up the project if he let me use the bike.

So Thomas, Jordan, Kent, and I all tinkered with it and made some bitchin' parts. It sort of turned out like something a touring bike racer from the 1940s or 1950s might own. It looked like it had aftermarket parts on it when there wasn't such a thing back then. We made a stainless-steel rack for the back fender, I made some stainless pipes for it, and we did an oil tank. We made a lot of nice parts that all worked really well together. When we took it to Cottonwood, Arizona, for the magazine's build-off event, the kids really checked it out and looked it over close because it wasn't the most whiz-bang bike there. We had a little trailer and truck with a little pop-up and Indian Larry and Leroy Thompson had big trucks. People were lined up for Indian Larry T-shirts, but when it came down to the voting and we won that thing, it was great.

One of the Salinas Boys' more recent bikes was this '41 Flathead for custom car builder Kent Kozera. Cole credits Jordan Skow for the sheet metal. *Max Trono,* Kustom *magazine*

Ken Benzo of Moro Bay went through the engine, which was in remarkably good order. *Max Trono*, Kustom *magazine*

Kozera requested the rack over the rear fender to haul belongings on trips. It was formed from stainless by former Salinas Boy Thomas Torjeson. The fender came from builder Chica; the seat is courtesy of Duane Ballard. *Max Trono*, Kustom *magazine*

The upswept stainless pipes and oil lines were also Cole's handiwork. *Max Trono*, Kustom *magazine*

Hot rod paint legend and longtime Cole Foster supporter Rod Powell sprayed the gold paint and laid on the stripes and lightning bolt motif. The bars, grips, headlight, dash, and gauges were the work of Cole and the shop. *Max Trono,* Kustom *magazine*

The Flattie's charm is its lack of knock-you-over-the-head parts. Instead, you have Powell's tasteful paint, a number of vintage parts, and tasteful custom-fabricated pieces crafted by folks who were all on the same page. *Max Trono*, Kustom *magazine*

Opposite: Electric start is superfluous to the design when you have a perfectly good kick. Cole strikes a classic pose alongside his '52 Panhead. *The Flyin' Dutchman, a.k.a. Maurice Van den Tillaard*

Cole's '52 Panhead earned the name "Dusty Rose" on one Internet board. Cole concocted the "mutt" satin from a number of colors he had laying around the shop. This was the bike, in its basket-case phase, that Cole originally considered as a donor for the Smoke Out West build-off. *David Perry*

MOON ROCKET

After Kirk Hammett's car, Susan and I moved, and I needed to do a bike. I had an old roller that I did for Custom Chrome, a frame and wheels and so forth, and I finally found some time to tinker on it. I love drag bikes like the Boris Murray Triumph with the café fairing on the front. They sat low and the fairings were fiberglass because they'd crash and just slap another one on. But on the street that fiberglass would last only a couple weeks before it would start cracking. I always wanted to play with aluminum more, so I made a full aluminum fairing for it, along with a gas tank, an oil tank, the fender, and a bunch of nice little parts.

It's not the most agile road bike—it's a dinosaur underneath those clothes. But period drag bikes were pretty in the front and business in the back, too, so that's exactly how I did the bike. It's like how Top Fuel cars went from bare tubing to pretty bodies. I didn't want to just make a Harley café racer, for example, because such a thing never existed. I think the bike shows a lot of craftsmanship, and if I'm guilty of being different, so be it.

Opposite: Cole readies the Moon Rocket for Paso Robles the night before departing, May 2007. *Peter Vincent*

The Moon Rocket arrives at Paso, May 2007. *Peter Vincent*

With the attention-grabbing Moon Rocket, Cole went back to one of his first inspirations: drag racing. In this case, though, it was more drag bikes like Boris Murray's Triumph than it was 1960s Top Fuelers. *Mike Chase*

Opposite: Cole came up with the Moon Rocket's stunning Honda-inspired fairing. "I always wanted to play with aluminum more," he says. He purchased the glass first, and then let the metalwork take shape. Underneath, Cole used a light and compact springer frontend. *Mike Chase*

Above: In addition to the fairing, Cole fabricated the tank, fender, and headers, and cast the oil tank. "It's not the most agile road bike," he says. "It's kind of a dinosaur underneath those clothes." As with the Blue Bike, the belt drive was cut down to a more compact width. *Mike Chase*

"Period drag bikes were pretty in the front and business in the back," Cole says, "That's exactly how I did this bike."
Mike Chase

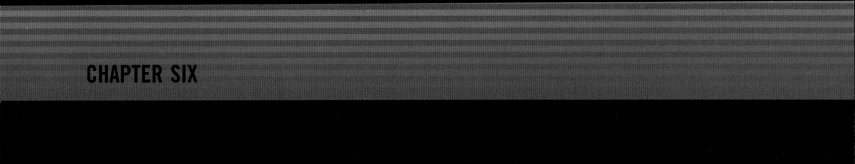

CHAPTER SIX

SUSAN

When I did the episodes of *Popular Hot Rodding* and *Corbin's Ride On*, the associate producer I always dealt with at the production company was a gal named Susan. If they were doing a bike show, she'd call and ask if I had anything new. So, I established a rapport with her on the phone, and I thought she was the girl that was on the set of the *Popular Hot Rodding* shoot. I was always talking to her on the phone like we had met. She probably just thought I was nuts.

Cole, Susan, and the '54 Bel Air, the car that first earned Cole and Salinas Boys national acclaim. *Zap Teshima*

Pat, Cole, and Susan Foster with Mooneyes owner Shige Suganuma at the Moon Café, Yokahama, December 2004. *Cole & Susan Foster collection*

Opposite: Cole credits Susan for promoting the business and making it run smoothly, freeing him to do what he does best. *Dave "DeLuxe" Wiltgen*

When I got to Dallas with the Blue Bike for the *Corbin's* shoot, I called Susan thinking it was the lady from the set of the previous shoot. I wasn't attracted to her or anything, I just thought she was nice, and I was bored, sitting in a hotel room. She said she was going out with some girlfriends and invited me along. I ended up at a restaurant waiting for her with her friends. Well, this knockout blonde came walking in and they all said, "Hey, Susan." I said, "That's not Susan," but insisted, "Yeah, that's Susan." I think I said, "Well, she's beautiful." What a weird surprise. I was drawn to her.

So we ended up laughing about it, and I spent a few days in Dallas. We hung out quite a bit and became friends. After I came home, she would call, but it wouldn't always be about cars. We started a long-distance romance.

Before I met Susan, every girl I ever dated hated what I did. But cars and bikes are my work, and besides the project I'm currently working on, I always have projects going in my head and I'm always looking forward to the next thing. I never sat around a day in my life, and I don't even know what the word "bored" means. I feel like the clock's ticking and I better hit it now.

I set up my life so that I could do whatever I wanted, and I've never really had a boss, but I'm sure I've paid for that in some ways. I've been poor, but I see the world through different eyes than most people. I guess I'm no different than some that came before me—beatniks, surfers, bikers, punk rockers, and maybe even hip-hop culture. But I guess it's about breaking something down to its simplest form and not listening to the B.S. That's what I try to do.

I've been with women who have really handicapped me. Mentally they caged me, and maybe I even submitted. I could have had a pyramid to build, but I was expected to sit on the couch and watch TV. That totally went against my nature, because I never have been one to do that, not when that thing inside is calling me. I can tell you that Susan is the first woman who actually shared my vision. Maybe she's a little more bohemian, more of a free spirit, which is interesting, because she comes from a background where she could have gone to medical school or law school, but I think she saw the world through different eyes, too. It's fun to share that with someone who wants to climb the same mountain.

Trinkets and baubles. A still life from the old shop space. *The Flyin' Dutchman, a.k.a. Maurice Van den Tillaard*

We had a long-distance thing going on at first, and since we were both getting out of long relationships, I think we were a little hesitant for a big commitment. But we had fun when we saw each other, and it wasn't lost on me that it's hard to find a girl who even tolerates what I do, let alone one who admired and was interested in my work.

When Susan finally decided to get out of Indianapolis, where she was working for Speed Channel, she really didn't know where she was going to go. So I said, "Why don't you send your things to my place, and I'll store them for you." She didn't have a ton of stuff, just some belongings and her little '65 Ford Caliente 411 four-speed. I said, "Just come here and stay with me for a couple weeks until you decide what to do. It'll be a free place." I really wasn't sure

that she would stay any longer than a month, but she's been here ever since and it's been amazing.

Susan, God bless her, put up with staying in my loft, which was above my old shop, for three years. A bachelor could live up there, but there were no windows. It was like a cave, and the poor girl was used to having gardens and dogs and a normal life. I'm glad we were eventually able to get out of there and give her the normalcy she deserves because she sure has helped me in more ways than I can count.

Because Susan was a television producer, it was natural for her to take what I had started and really put things into motion. She built our website, and because she had a lot of contacts in the business world, was a

Cole and Susan's roomier, more comfortable digs—with windows! *Peter Vincent*

great promoter. But besides that, just having someone who's truly on your team and can say the things to people that you can't—it's like having a manager. She's freed me from the tasks I can't stand—the paperwork, billing, and even ordering parts. She increased my business tenfold. I'm not the greatest businessman in the world. It was always difficult for me to charge what I was worth. Since I never had money myself, when I looked at what I was billing customers, I'd always put myself in their place, and think, "Man, that seems like a lot." So I always made concessions on bills and I'd end up cheating myself out of money. I still might not be the greatest at writing down how many hours I actually work. For instance, if I'm out in the shop for twelve

hours I might write down five or six, but now at least I get paid for that, and what a difference that has made.

There were definitely some women over the years that wanted to get married, but I just never had that feeling. It's hard when someone keeps telling you that you'll never amount to anything. I'm glad I didn't get stuck in one of those relationships, because when you're in one like I am now, it's wide open for me to build this building as tall as I want. It's the freedom I've always strived for. My family was getting a little worried that I was going to end up "old bachelor Cole," but I pulled it off, and I couldn't be happier. I've got a best friend, a lover, and a true partner. She does a great job of just shoveling coal to the monster so that I keep chugging along.

Above: In Venice, summer 2007.
Cole & Susan Foster collection

Left: Jesolo Beach, Italy,
welcomes Cole, summer 2007,
with friend Max Busato. *Cole
& Susan Foster collection*

Opposite: On the set of Miller
Beer commercial shoot, 2004.
Cole & Susan Foster collection

and becomes really good at what he does, then he has to leave home. It's a heartbreaker. I don't know if I'll ever really get used to that. It's been a changing cast of characters, and I guess I'm the only common denominator.

For the most part, I still have a great relationship with those guys, but it's been hard. It's a weird business. I think of myself as an artist, but I've had help creating the artwork. There are parts of each piece of art that other people have been involved in, but sometimes only my name gets mentioned in the press. Unfortunately, that's just the way it is sometimes.

Of all the people who have come and gone, about half of them have gone on to do other things, but the other half have made building their profession. Sometimes I know they won't stay forever. Before Corey Conyers worked with me, he'd never been out of Kansas. He came out for three years and helped me build Sal Tarantino's truck. We hung out day in and day out. He always owned a house in Wichita, and after three years, it was time for him to go home.

Another kid I worked closely with was Aaron Elliott, who started here when he was a kid and now is a fabricator. Aaron is the nephew of an upholstery guy named Ronnie Burke. I had watched Aaron since he was about fifteen, doing things like chopping a truck outside his uncle's shop during the summer. He had tons of ambition and was super brave, but he needed some skills. When he finally moved up here from Sacramento, I scooped him up and brought him in. He helped out tremendously on the Hammett '36. It was really tough when he left as well.

In the last couple of years, I've worked with a young guy I really like named Jordan Skow. He's laid back and even-keeled, a very intelligent son of a pastor who was home-schooled. He lives on the same piece of property as the rest of his family, and his dad has antique cars that were handed down from his great-grandfather. I know he won't be a Salinas Boy forever, but when he leaves, I know he'll always be a friend and an associate, because he's one of the people who can enjoy the fruits of what we've all accomplished together. When I get invited to do appearances and things, my guys are always welcome to come with me. I don't treat people like they're my personal assistants. It's more like an entourage, and they can enjoy it, which Jordan does because he's very good with people.

THE SALINAS BOYS

In the beginning, it was just me and my friends—Job Stevens, Todd and Chad Gravelle, and Sean—at the shop. They're like regulars on a soap opera—they come and go, but for the most part are still around. Even Job has never been here for a long stretch of time. It's a loose thing—if he ever wants to come and work, he knows he can. And I can still call him and say, "Hey, you need to come and check something out," because I trust him and I know I'll get complete honesty. I think everyone needs that person in their life.

Over the years, I've had to get used to the fact that some kids just come, learn what they need to learn, and then go. When you bring a guy in and build a relationship, it's kind of like having a kid. You nurture him, he grows

The latest heartbreak was Thomas Torjeson, who came all the way from Norway back in 2004. It's nice to get someone who already has skills, and that was Thomas. He was probably the best all-around Salinas Boy. I think it was hard for him because he's a guy who can do it all, just not in Norway—there's just no scene over there. When he first told me he wanted to come over here to work, I advised him against it. It represented a huge commitment and what if he couldn't stand me or it wasn't what he thought it would be? Eventually I told him, "Why don't you just come over for a couple months, see how you like it, and then make a decision after that?" I picked him up from the airport and after a twenty-hour airplane ride, he started right in on the *Biker Build-Off* episode. He stayed quite awhile, eventually moving his whole family over from Norway.

I think that with some people it bothers them that magazines come here and want to talk to me, or that my name comes up exclusively on a project that they were a big part of. I always try to let writers know what everyone's role in a project was, but I'm not always able to control what makes it to print, and I can't help it when some kid wants to take a picture with me at a car show and doesn't know who they are. They get the feeling that they didn't get enough credit, but it's really out of my hands. When someone does a nice job, I tell them, I tell the customer, hell, I tell it to anyone who will listen. But if that's not enough for a guy, I can't help it. Unfortunately, that was the case with Thomas. Before there's bad blood, they should go and do their own thing, because I don't want to be responsible for someone's dream not happening. If someone wants to play under my roof, they have to be secure with themselves and take pride in it what they do. I don't claim to do everything, and I try to give credit where credit's due.

I think I have a good grasp on my ego, and I don't beat my chest. I think I'm subtle, just like with my work. In the beginning, nobody, especially magazines or TV shows, cared about what we were doing. Now bikes and cars are popular in our culture and there's a sought-after group of craftsmen whose work is celebrated as a lost American art form. Among those people, I'll probably never have the biggest crowds, but then again, it just wouldn't feel right.

Cole surveys the scene with the Hammett '36 and the Kozera '41 Flathead. *Max Trono, Kustom* magazine

DESIGN

Growing up around racing—specifically drag racing—has had a lot of influence on my design. Drag racing is so cool because the early cars had just the bare essentials—it was just form following function. A circa-1968 front-engine Top Fuel car is absolutely the baddest machine on the planet as far as I'm concerned.

To quote my dad, "It's like a great white shark or a jet fighter . . . you know when you see it that it's something you don't want to mess with." A front-engine Top Fuel car is all business. It's just a man sitting on a motor. There's a simplistic mechanical beauty there, and when I do a motorcycle, I keep that in mind. It's just a man sitting on a motor, so when I make parts, I know that everything's going to show. It's exciting because there is so much history—racing and street—to draw on that a design can go in a couple of different directions, but I seem to always be drawn back to the racer side because of that raw essence.

As a kid I liked some choppers, but those were sort of hippie bikes to me. I remember seeing those bikes going down the freeway, but I liked the bikes that the guys rode in the dirt, the same guys who would do wheelies down

A bewigged Pat Foster dons his double's costume before climbing behind the wheel of *Jade Grenade* for the filming of the famous 2004 Dodge Hemi commercial. *Cole & Susan Foster collection*

the street for me. The early biker movies didn't have those really long bikes, but when people think of a chopper today, that's what they always picture. When I think of a chopper, I think hot rod, because that was originally a car broken down to its bare essentials. They were made light for performance, and if a part was unnecessary, it stayed in the garage. The lighter, the faster, and the less crap you have on it, the less there is to break. With motorcycles, that's how it is for me.

When I started doing bikes, I looked at other people's and wondered, "Why do they have all this crap on them?" My approach was, "Okay, this needs a battery," so I would just mount a battery in the simplest way possible. It doesn't need a cover on the box, and it especially doesn't need a box covering the box. Aftermarket catalogs make covers for everything—every bolt, every component. They have a dozen different ways to hide everything, but I find beauty in mechanical things, so I do the total opposite. If something has a little toggle switch, I don't care if I see the back of it. It's rare to see a soldered wire with wrap on it. That, to me, is beauty unto itself. I just let things speak for themselves and stay as far away as I can from covering anything. Let it be beautiful for what it is. I think people get that.

I'd like to say that holds true for everything I do, but it does depend on the project. The bike I built for Custom Chrome, for instance, was a different way of thinking, because it had to be more about beauty than function. When I take on a project, I try to get into character, to put myself into the original designer's shoes. I think of the guys who drew up the 1936 Ford or the 1950s Fords. I bet that they had meetings and their designs got watered down. Probably some of the greatest ideas in the world hit the trash can. Since I don't have the bureaucracy to deal with, the red tape that those guys had to go through, I can make it however I want to.

I don't want to lose the essence of what something is, so when I build a V-twin, for example, I want it to be all V-twin. If it's a '36 Ford, I want it to look like a '36 Ford. I don't want to put a mask on anything. I want it to be what it is, but break it down a little, make it a bit rawer, and maybe improve on the line or the style statement it makes. Maybe the manufacturer missed it and I can improve it. But if I can't improve it, I try not to make changes just for the sake of changing things.

For years the feeling was that if you're a car guy, you can't do bikes, which is funny because if you look at custom bike culture over the last forty years, it's mostly been car guys who have upped the ante. When Roth got into bikes, he changed things for sure, and people paid attention. Bob Dron was another car guy who stepped into bikes, and Lil' John Buttera changed V-twins probably more than anyone. So, when people say, "You're a car guy, is it hard doing bikes?" I say, "You're asking the wrong guy," because this is easy for me. Go ask the big bike guys to build cars, and let's see how that works out. You don't see that switchover often, and there's a reason for that. What would cars built by some of these bike guys look like? Would they have swords coming out the back? It would be remarkable to see.

I could go on for days about the custom bike world, because it's like a Saturday morning cartoon show at these bike shows. It gets hard for me to walk through the shows with a straight face because I see some of the most ridiculous ideas on the planet. But if I don't stop and look, I'm an "asshole," so I have to act like I'm looking at everyone's bikes and nod to them. And then there's the bigger question: "Who's buying it?" I do know they're not looking at history, and certainly not at racing.

It was hard for me when I started doing bikes because I came out of left field and no one was doing what I was doing. I couldn't believe that, because motorcycles are so American, and what builders were doing with them was just embarrassing. Grown men with beards and tattoos, real badasses, riding cartoon character motorcycles that looked like Bugs Bunny designed them. You'd see things welded onto the bikes that were like bridges to nowhere, parts that didn't do anything. When I asked what they were doing, they would say, "Just trying to be different, bro." That was a constant reminder to me to never try to be different just for the sake of it.

THE SINNERS

For the last ten years I've run with a bunch of guys called The Sinners. At first nobody knew who they were—they were just guys I met through Rico Fodrey, one of my closest friends. If you look in an old hot rod magazine, Sinners was always one of the examples used in ads for club plaques. But they apparently met some older guys

In the old shop with fellow Sinner Rico Fodrey. "I've never met a group of guys that I instantly liked and had such an immediate rapport with." *Cole & Susan Foster collection*

Sinners Kutty Noteboom and Job Stevens, San Francisco, 2000. *Cole & Susan Foster collection*

With Dad outside the Wally Parks NHRA Motorsports Museum, February 2007. *Cole & Susan Foster collection*

who handed the name down to them and told them to reopen the club. Jason Jessee, Job Stevens, and I were hanging out with them one time, and they just asked, "You guys want to be Sinners?" Even though I always stayed away from clubs, this was more of a brotherhood.

I think what really clinched it for me were these two guys from the club, big three-hundred-pound biker types with beards, who French kissed at Paso Robles the year before right in front of all the rockabilly kids, which just scared them to death. I had seen photos of Hells Angels kissing, and I thought, "These guys are badass. I've got to hang out with them." Rico is the "King of The Sinners," and there's also Kutty Noteboom, who's pretty well known, Jeff Decker, Chopper Dave, musician James Intveld, and Danny Takahashi, among others. And they build bitchin' bikes. I've never met a group of guys that I instantly liked and had such an immediate rapport with.

IN THE END . . .

There might be a segment of people who think what I do is ridiculous, but I don't understand why. Like I've said, I'm not doing anything earth-shattering, just the right thing, keeping all the essence, and breaking things down to where they are free. That's it. I've tried to run my life the same way—just keep everything simple and do what's right for me.

I guess it all boils down to what my dad instilled in me from a young age: "Hey, kid . . . don't fuck up." I've had a lot of fun, but I've always been careful. It's rare to live on your own terms like I have and make it to forty years old without a few kids and a couple of divorces under your belt, or worse yet, a couple years in the big house. Through it all, I've always cherished my friends and my freedom. I'm thankful to be able to do these cars and bikes and live free.

AS TIME PASSES AND MY SON COLE'S TALENTS ARE DISCOVERED *by anyone who pays attention to things mechanical, my pride in him as a builder and human being, also grows.*

I have read many times that the acorn didn't fall far from the tree in reference to Cole's abilities. The truth is that pretty much the only thing I passed on to him was the ability to recognize excellence. As a racer and builder, I was able to expose him to both the finest and the worst work being done in my chosen field of professional drag racing. I was too busy trying to make a living and advance my career to be of much hands-on help to a young son, who wanted desperately to learn the secrets from his dad. He forged on and learned the hand skills needed to create the things he saw in his head. It had to be frustrating to see what he was able to envision and not be able to bring it all to fruition, especially when he had a father who did the things he so wanted to do but was not very available.

Forge ahead he did, teaching himself the skills he needed to create not just hot rods and motorcycles, but art in its purest form. In our case, the acorn fell farther from the tree than most would ever believe. Cole has skills that I can only dream of having. I build cars. Cole, like the old masters in the art world, creates more than just cars and bikes. His work will become more important with time and will live on long after my stuff is laying at a swap meet somewhere.

I think Cole's early work was done more to get his dad's approval than to make money or be famous. Getting my approval was no easy task. I could find fault with even the smallest detail on his projects, but I felt that if he earned my accolades, his work would become world-class. The rest is history and it's still being written— and will be for many years to come.

—Pat Foster, a proud father

Pat Foster with Cole and Rico Fodrey at the 2007 Pomona internationals. The car is Paul Candies' 1966 Top Fueler. *Cole & Susan Foster collection*

AFTERWORD

AGAINST THE MERETRICIOUS MASSES

Arthur Coleman Foster and I grew up only a few dozen 101 Freeway exits from each other: he in the Valley and I on the L.A./Ventura County line. Our fathers would bring us to the Irwindale or Lions drag strips on varied weekends, as the NHRA called his dad and the Antique Nationals called mine. We skated the same parks, surfed the same beaches, and saw the same bands at the same venues. Our stars clearly crossed, but our paths never did.

It took someone from across the world to bring us together. Giuseppe Roncen, the editor of an Italian motorcycle magazine, felt something fresh was coming out of California. He was growing tired of the current robotic/transformer trend in Euro bikes and could see no end to America's love of fat tires and long forks. He noticed a departure occurring with a car customizer, skater Jason Jessee, and a sculptor. Giuseppe and I meet in Thousand Oaks, grabbed my pop's '39 Zephyr Custom, and headed north. It had been more than a decade since I'd seen Jason, and I'd never met Cole Foster. The old Salinas Boys shop, in a row of industrial buildings on Burton Avenue, is where we met.

When I first laid eyes on Cole—not his cars or bikes, but his person—the lyrics of the Warren Zevon song "Werewolves of London" came to mind: "You better stay away from him, he'll rip your lungs out, Jim" and "his hair was perfect."

In fact, his hair is perfect, and that is one of Cole's biggest problems. The world can see dreadlocks and mohawks, but they can't see perfection. You see, Cole grew up before racecars became rolling billboards for laundry detergent. He knows that less is less. I hate the cliché "less is more." Think of a dragster: less weight, less distraction, less drag . . . just less.

The mouth-breathing public is always eyeing the flash. They love the meretricious. If one skull is cool, then they'll airbrush 400 of them in a purple ghost flame that never ends. Cole is subtle, with a discriminating eye and a great understanding of line and proportion. He uses phases such as "form follows function" and never loses sight of the fact that he is working on a motorcycle or car and not a space shuttle. He knows not to hide functionality, but to beautify it. Harry Miller understood that, and every guy who ever pulled the fenders off a '32 Ford did so because the hood and grille related to the frame rails like a Miller. The frame horns came past the grille and you had a quick and easy way to make your ordinary Ford look like a racecar. But who knows that or even cares? Ed Roth's name is dropped more than Harry Miller's.

Cole knows how much racing can influence customizing and follows suit. He worries about the fit and finish rather than disguising the part. He won't betray a car either, sending it in a direction it wasn't meant to go. How many times have you seen a concept car or prototype and said to yourself "Why didn't they leave it alone?" Because Cole's hands aren't tied by business bureaucracy, he can strip off the elements of industry regulation that smothered the original designer. His intent is to refine every element of his project through simplicity.

If you are seeking popularity, strive for mediocrity. If you are Cole Foster and integrity is important to you, it may take a lifetime to get the recognition you deserve.

When you really look at old car and bike magazines—and Cole has studied thousands—you'll discover that most of the stuff in the "good old days" was junk, just like it is today. Journalists are starved for material, so they keep on writing articles about '32 Fords and '57 Chevys. If a journalist even owns a custom car, I enjoy looking at it, and I usually discover that although the guy is articulate, he lacks that discriminating eye. He'll write a great piece on Cole's work, and I'll think, "Right on, he gets it." Then in the next issue, he is as flattering to the kook's car with flames, checkers, scallops, twenty-three skulls, and nineteen pairs of dice.

Cole is understated in a world that needs to be hit over the head with a sledgehammer to take notice. Don't get me wrong, Cole would love to bash 'em, but all he has is a ball-peen hammer.

XOXO!
Jeff Decker

The Decker Special K bike. *The Flyin' Dutchman, a.k.a. Maurice Van den Tillaard*

ACKNOWLEDGMENTS

I WOULD LIKE TO THANK MANY PEOPLE for making this book a reality, including Dennis Pernu at Motorbooks for his patience and guidance, and Crazy Mike LaVella for puttin' my rants onto paper and dealing with my chaotic schedule.

A big thanks to my beautiful wife Susan for putting up with my B.S. mood swings and late nights that I like to call "life with an artist," not to mention taking care of all the business functions so I can just create. She is a big inspiration!

Pictures tell a story, and without the contributions of photographers from around the world, this book wouldn't be a reality. Thank you, Laurent Bagnard, Bo Bertilsson, Mike Chase, Jesus Espinoza, The Flyin' Dutchman (a.k.a. Maurice Van den Tillaard), Rob Fortier, David Perry, Giuseppe Roncen, Zap Teshima, Max Trono, Peter Vincent, Dave "DeLuxe' Wiltgen, and Adam Wright. These guys have made me and my work look so good!

To my mom, Carolynn, my father, Pat, my brother, Dan, and his wife, Kari, thanks for bringing me up, teaching me hard work and honesty, and giving me words of wisdom when they count.

Nothing I do would have been out of the ordinary a hundred years ago. Craftsmanship and style is becoming a lost art. Not one tool, technique, or bit of knowledge would exist today without those who came before me. I'm amazed on a daily basis by what mankind figured out and built before power tools, building beautiful pieces by candlelight.

I can't forget the heroes whose automotive magic I've been lucky enough to soak up: my father, Pat Foster, Lil' John Buttera, Bobby Walden, Jimmy Shine, Marcos Garcia, John Aiello, Billy F Gibbons, Jerry "Uncle E," Bill Manger, Greg Lazzerini, Jim Hume, Bill Carter, Tom Hanna, Corey Conyers, Benny Negranze, John Glaspy, JW and Shaylor, the Kennedy brothers, Kenny Youngblood, Don Kirby, Dave Smith, Rod Powell, Buck and George Thomas, the Gravelle Family, Mike Hubbard, Bill Stewart, Job Stevens, Jason Jessee, Rico Fodrey, Kutty Noteboom, Jesse Cruz, Don Orosco, Ron Covell, Steve Moal, Dan Woods, and John Fleliciano, to name but a few.

Another big thanks to all my customers who let me do my thing: Henry Gong, Sal Tarantino, Kirk and Lani Hammett, Dan Woods, Mike Ness, Steve Veltri and Custom Chrome, Kent Kozera, Jerry Wilkerson, and everyone else!

Finally, to all the Salinas Boys past and present, thank you.

Cole Foster,
Salinas, California

WRITING THIS BOOK WITH COLE truly has been one of the more interesting chapters in my life. Going into it, I knew that because we were more or less the same age and came out of the same scene, that I was capable of pulling it off, but as we got things rolling, it was remarkable how much we actually had in common. Beyond obvious things like growing up with skateboarding and punk rock, we shared incredibly similar views on virtually everything that matters: loyalty to friends and family, working with integrity, and a healthy distrust of anything we perceived as authority. By the end of the interviews, we were actually ending each other's sentences. After spending so much time with Cole, Susan, and the rotating cast of characters that round out the Salinas Boys, I simply couldn't do anything less than the best job I was capable of.

So I approached this book in the same way that Cole takes on building a car: I took my time. I reckoned that you shouldn't rush something that will be out there forever. However, in the world of publishing, where the deadline is king, that attitude is nothing short of nightmarish for a publisher. So thanks go out to the tolerant folks at Motorbooks, especially our editor, Dennis Pernu. They say that guy in the Bible named Job had a lot of patience, but trust me: he has nothing on this guy. I'd also like to thank the dedicated staff at my own publication, *Gearhead* magazine, because even though I appear to drop off the face of the earth whenever I take on a project like this, they are always standing by, ready to go right back to work whenever I am. I am one lucky guy to be surrounded by such loyal and talented people, and I know it.

Mike LaVella,
Oakland, California

INDEX